A LITTLE CHILD'S FIRST COMMUNION

INTRODUCTION TO THE SPIRITUAL WAY

By MOTHER BOLTON
Religious of The Cenacle

*Associate Professor, Department of Education,
for the Teaching of Christian Doctrine,
Fordham University, New York City.*

ILLUSTRATIONS BY L. JAMBOR

St. Augustine Academy Press
HOMER GLEN, ILLINOIS

Imprimi Potest
FR. MATHIAS FAUST, O. F. M.,
Minister Provincialis.

Nihil Obstat
ARTHUR J. SCANLAN, S. T. D.,
Censor Librorum.

Imprimatur
✠ PATRICK CARDINAL HAYES,
Archbishop of New York.

New York, July 1, 1935.

This work was originally published in 1935 by St. Anthony Guild Press, as six individual booklets. This edition, reprinted in 2021 by St. Augustine Academy Press, combines all six in one.
ISBN: 978-1-64051-112-5

A LITTLE CHILD'S FIRST COMMUNION

BOOK ONE: Page 1
God Is Love.
Creation: God's Gifts of Love.

BOOK TWO: Page 23
God Is Truth.
Our First Parents.
A Promise by the God of Truth.
The Prophets.
God's Own Son.

BOOK THREE: Page 57
The Mother of God's Own Son.
The Story of Saint Joseph.
The Life of Jesus.
The Blessed Trinity.
The Commandments.

BOOK FOUR: Page 111
Jesus' Church.
The Holy Mass.

BOOK FIVE: Page 157
The Sacraments: Baptism, Penance, Holy Eucharist

A PREPARATION FOR CONFIRMATION

BOOK SIX   Page 211
The Sacraments: Extreme Unction Holy Orders, Matrimony

A PREPARATION FOR FIRST HOLY COMMUNION

SIX BOOKS IN THE SERIES
EACH BOOK COMPLETE IN ITSELF

F O R E W O R D

As every little baptized child is a "temple of the Living God," when a parent or teacher is teaching Christ's principles to one of these little children, that parent or teacher is dealing directly with God. For that parent or teacher is co-operating with God within His temple, helping to make brighter and stronger God's image and likeness within the child.

That many parents and teachers may co-operate with God in helping to make brighter and stronger God's image and likeness in many, many little children is the prayer of

The Author.

Approved by the National Center of The Confraternity of Christian Doctrine

STORIES ABOUT GIFTS OF LOVE

O YOU give your love to some people?

Do some people give their love to you?

There is Someone Who gives all people greater love than anyone else can give.

Book One of "A Little Child's First Communion" tells about The One Who gives all the love in the world.

✦ ✦ ✦ ✦

HERE is a story about a boy called Tom. Would you like to read the story?

For a long time Tom wanted a dog of his own. No one but his sister Ann

1

A STORY ABOUT TOM

knew that Tom wanted a dog. And Ann could not buy Tom a dog because she did not have any money.

Tom's birthday was the seventh of March. When he came home from school on his birthday he heard a dog barking. He thought it was some visitor's dog; but when he looked at the dog's collar it said: "Bobby. Owned by Tom White, twenty-eight Park Street."

Tom did not know who gave him Bobby. All that his father and mother said, was — "Someone who loves you very much gave you Bobby."

Tom knew that his father and mother had much more love for him than other people had. So he was sure that Bobby was a gift from one of them.

Can you tell a story about something which you like because it was given to you by someone who loves you very much?

✤ ✤ ✤ ✤

A STORY ABOUT ANN

ONE DAY after school, as Ann was opening the door of her own little room, she heard a strange sound. She listened. She heard tick, tick, tick.

She opened the door. She looked about to see what made the tick, tick, tick. She saw something on the table which she had not seen there before.

What do you think Ann saw on the table in her little room? She saw a pretty clock. Near the clock was a small piece of paper and on the paper was written: "For Ann. With much love."

Ann was not sure who had given her the clock, but she knew that her father and mother had much more love for her than other people had. So Ann was happy to think that the clock was a gift from them.

Can you tell a story about something that you did for your father and mother because you loved them?

MAKE-BELIEVE WORLDS

LET US make believe that James, John, William, Michael and Paul lived in five different make-believe worlds.

James lived in a make-believe world where there was not a dog or a horse or a cow. In this make-believe world there were no animals at all. So James said: "Oh, how I wish there were live things running around on the earth so that I could see them and keep them with me and play with them!"

William lived in a make-believe world where there was not a tree or a flower or any grass. There was nothing in that world but the ground and rocks and stones.

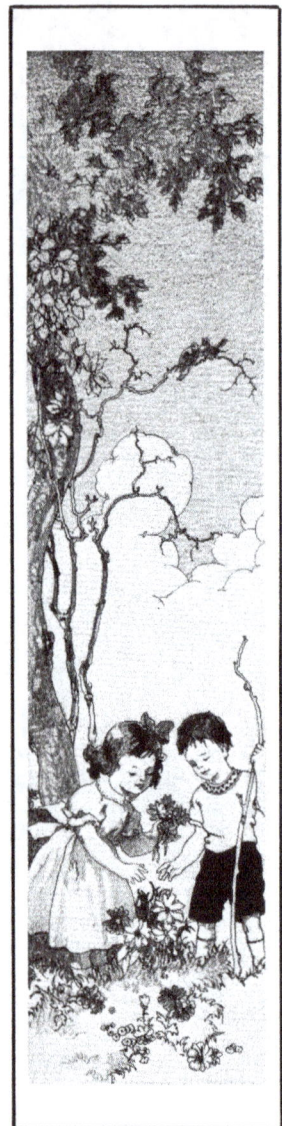

What do you think he said? William said: "Oh, I wish the ground could be covered with something soft and green and I wish there could be something to make it shady when the sun shines, and I wish there were some pretty red and yellow and violet things growing everywhere on the green!"

John lived in a make-believe world where there was no moon or stars at night and where there was no sun at all. This make-believe world was dark and cold. So John said: "Oh, I wish there could be something to give light all day long, and something to keep me warm, and I wish there could be pretty bright lights in the sky at night!"

Michael lived in a make-believe world that was all land. In this make-believe world there was no ocean or lake or river or pond. So Michael wished and wished that he could wade and swim and sail and feel the cool breezes when it was hot.

Paul lived in a make-believe world where there were no fathers or mothers or brothers or sisters. No people were there at all. Paul said: "Oh, I wish there were people here who knew me and took care of me and did good things for me. I wish there were people here who loved me!"

PROJECT WORK

Draw the five make-believe worlds.
Under each picture write a sentence telling what is missing in that make-believe world.

STORIES ABOUT SOMEONE WHOM WE HAVE NOT SEEN

TOM AND Ann read about the five boys and the make-believe worlds.

When they read about James who lived in the make-believe world where there was not a dog or a horse or a cow, they said:

"**Someone is good!**

"Someone has given us dogs and horses and cows and all kinds of animals.

"**Someone must love us very much!**"

When they read about William who lived in the make-believe world where there were no trees or flowers or grass and where there was nothing but dirt and rocks and stones, they said: "Someone has given us trees and flowers and grass.

"**Someone must love us very much!**"

When they read about John who lived in the make-believe world where there was no moon at night or not even a star and where there was no sun all day long, Tom said: "I would not like to live in a world like that." And Ann said:

"**Someone is good to us!**

"Someone has given us a moon and stars to light the night and a sun to make the day bright and to keep us warm.

"**Someone must love us very much!**"

When they read about Michael who lived in the make-believe world where there was land but no ocean, or lake or river or pond, they said:

"Someone is very good!

"Someone has given us ponds and rivers and lakes and the big oceans.

"Someone must love us very much!"

When they read about Paul who lived in the make-believe world where there were no fathers or mothers or brothers or sisters and no one to take care of him and do good things for him, they said:

"Someone is very good to us!

"Someone has given us fathers and mothers and other people who know us and do good things for us.

"Someone must love us very much!"

Then Ann said to Tom: "I wish we could see THE ONE Who gave us the moon, the stars, the sun, the animals, the trees, the flowers, the grass, the rivers, the lakes, the oceans, our fathers and mothers and all the people who love us."

Project Work

Find pictures of the things that are missing in each make-believe world. Paste these pictures in your First Communion Notebook, or on project pages. And under each picture write what Tom and Ann said when they read about that make-believe world.

WHO CARES FOR LITTLE CHILDREN

Music by
CORNELIA S. CRANE

Who fills the sky with stars so bright?

Who keeps all chil-dren in His care?

Who gives us dai-ly warmth and light?

Whose love and gifts are ev-'ry-where?

Ask your father or mother to write your name in the blank spaces and to sign the page if you have done this work correctly.

............can tell what was missing in James' make-believe world, and what James said.

............can tell what was missing in William's John's, Michael's and Paul's make-believe worlds and what William, John, Michael and Paul said.

............can tell what Tom and Ann said when they read about James; about William; about John; about Michael; about Paul.

............can tell what Ann said about The One Who gave us all the good things we see in the world.

............can say or sing the verse: "Who Cares for Little Children."

............has finished the project work asked for on pages 7 and 11.

....
Parent's Signature

THE PRIEST'S STORY

On THE way to their First Communion class Tom and Ann were talking about the make-believe worlds.

Tom said to Ann: "Let us ask the priest to tell us more about The One Whom we cannot see."

✤ ✤ ✤ ✤

That night Tom and Ann told their mother what the priest had said to them. This is what they told their mother:

"God gave us the moon, the stars, the sun, the animals, the trees, the flowers, the rivers, the oceans, and our fathers and mothers. These are all God's gifts of love,

"FOR GOD IS LOVE.

"GOD IS ALSO THE GREAT GIVER OF LOVE.

"AND HE IS OUR FATHER.

"He is doing good things for us all the time. But the priest said that

"The very best thing God does for us is to give us

"OF HIS LOVE.

"He told us to ask God every day to give us more and more of His Love. For, he said,

"**When God's Love is in us, we are God's very dear children.**

"Then the priest gave us this little card with these prayers on it.

"He said that he knew you would help us to learn the Acts of Faith, Hope and Love."

AN ACT OF FAITH

O my God, I believe that You are my Father. I believe that You love me.

AN ACT OF HOPE

O my God, I hope that I shall always keep Your Love in me.

AN ACT OF LOVE

O my God and my Father, I love You. Please give me more and more of Your Love.

PAGE 16

ACTS OF FAITH, HOPE AND LOVE
Music by
CORNELIA S. CRANE

O God I be-lieve in Thy dear love for me; For from Thee comes all good in this world here be-low; Dearest God fill my heart with Thy Faith, Hope and Love, For Then ev-ery day in Thy fa-vor I'll grow.

A Test

There are six sentences in this test.

There are six words to be put into the sentences.

Pick out the right word for each space.

day	children	see
us	God	Love

1. All the good in the world comes from ....

2. We cannot .... The One Who gave us a father and mother and all good things.

3. The best thing that God does for us is to give us of His ....

4. God wants .... to love Him.

5. God wants us to ask Him every .... for more and more of His Love.

6. When God's Love is in us we are His very dear ....

Ask someone at home if you have picked out the right word for each space.

Write the sentences in your First Communion Notebook.

GOD IS ALL GOOD

Music by
CORNELIA S. CRANE

Dear God Thy gifts are ev-'ry-where
All that I have, all comes from Thee
But though Thou send-est man-y gifts,
Thy love is dear-est un-to me.

A Test

The first and last parts of six prayers are given in this test.

Ask someone at home if you have put the right parts of the prayers together.

.... You. Please give me more and more of Your Love.

.... my heart with Thy Faith, Hope and Love.

.... my Father. I believe that You love me.

.... believe in Thy dear Love for me.

.... that I shall always keep Your Love in me.

.... gifts are everywhere.

1. Dearest God, fill ....

2. O my God, I believe that You are ....

3. Dear God, Thy ....

4. O my God, I hope ....

5. O God, I ....

6. O my God and my Father, I love ....

Write these prayers in your First Communion Notebook or on project pages.

Ask your father or mother to write your name in the blank spaces and to sign the page if you have done this work correctly.

............can name ten of God's gifts of love.

............can tell which of God's gifts is the very best one.

............can tell the reason why God can give us greater love than any one else.

............knows what the priest told Tom and Ann to ask for every day.

............knows what makes us God's very dear children.

............can answer the next three questions.

What did you tell God when you said the Act of Faith?

What did you tell God when you said the Act of Hope?

When you said an Act of Love, what gift did you ask God to give you?

............knows the Acts of Faith, Hope and Love.

............can do the tests on pages 13, 18 and 20.

............has finished the project work asked for on pages 7 and 11.

............can say or sing the verses on pages 12, 17 and 19.

....
Parent's Signature

BOOK TWO

STORIES ABOUT PEOPLE WHO LOVED TRUTH.

Book One Told Us That
GOD IS THE GREAT GIVER OF LOVE
FOR
GOD IS ALL-LOVE.
GOD IS ALSO ALL-TRUTH
and
HE IS THE GREAT GIVER OF TRUTH.

The Stories in Book Two
are about people who loved God's Truth.
And one of these stories will tell you
about
THE ONE WHO LOVED TRUTH
MOST OF ALL.

Approved by the National Center of The Confraternity
of Christian Doctrine

TOM AND HIS MOTHER

ONE DAY Tom's mother made some cookies. She asked Tom to take a plate of the cookies to his aunt who lived on another street. On his way to his aunt's house, Tom met some big boys. They took the cookies from him and ate them.

Tom returned home and told his mother what had happened. But when Tom's mother asked the big boys why they took the cookies, they said: "We did not take the cookies. Tom ate them."

This made Tom's mother feel very sad. For she thought Tom had told her something which was not the truth. And she said to him:

"Tom, you know that every day when we say the Act of Faith together, we tell God that we believe HE IS OUR FATHER and that He loves us.

"And I have taught you that GOD IS ALL-LOVE.

"Today I want you to learn that GOD IS ALSO ALL-TRUTH.

"And, Tom, God wants His Truth in every boy and girl as well as in every man and woman.

"He gives us of His Love and Truth at the time of our Baptism.

"And this gift helps us **to act** like 'The God of Truth.' It helps us to love truth and to be truthful.

Tom Prayed to God

"IT MAKES US GOD'S OWN CHILDREN.

"And God wants all of His children **to keep** His Love and Truth in them.

"You know how much I love you, Tom, but I would rather have you die now than grow to be a man who has not kept God's Love and Truth in him."

The big boys had told Tom's mother that Tom was not truthful. But Tom was happy. For he knew that he was truthful. **And he was sure that God knew it, too.**

But Tom wanted his mother to be happy. So he asked God to make his mother know that

HE WAS A TRUE CHILD OF "THE GOD OF TRUTH"

AND THAT HE HAD NOT TOLD A LIE.

✦ ✦ ✦ ✦

A Test

1. Why was Tom's mother very sad?

2. What prayer did Tom and his mother say together every day?

3. What did Tom's mother say that she had taught him about God?

4. What else did Tom's mother want to teach him about God?

5. What gift does God give us at the time of our Baptism?

6. When do we become God's Own children?

7. Why was Tom happy even after the big boys had told a lie about him?

GOD LOVES THE TRUTH

Music by
CORNELIA S. CRANE

More than the world, God loves the truth,
He loves the truth-ful child I know; And
so I ask of God to-day To
keep me truth-ful as I grow.

THE STORY OF OUR FIRST PARENTS

I

THIS is a very important story.

The story tells about the first man and woman, Adam and Eve.

Their home was in a far-away country. The name of their home was Paradise. It was very beautiful.

All the people living upon the earth today and all the people who have ever lived upon the earth are the children of Adam and Eve. So we call this man and woman our first parents.

Our first parents were very holy. For God had given them of His Love and Truth.

They knew that they were the dear children of The Great Giver of Love and Truth.

They paid attention to God. And they loved Him. So all that they knew was good, beautiful and true.

AND THEY WERE VERY HAPPY.

This part of the story tells about our first parents when they were living in Paradise. Tell the story.

II

But one sad, sad day our first parents did not pay attention to God. And when they did not pay attention to God, they believed something which was not true.

PAGE 7

No Longer Holy

Then they did what they knew God did not want them to do. You see they did not give to God love and obedience. They disobeyed Him.

And after they had disobeyed God, everything was changed for them.

At that moment, first of all, they were

NO LONGER HOLY.

For they had turned away from the Great Giver of Love and Truth.

And, at once, they began to understand that they were

NO LONGER

THE DEAR CHILDREN

of The One Who is All-Love and All-Truth.

PAGE 8

After that, they could not live in Paradise any longer.

And from that time on they suffered from hard work, heat, cold and sickness.

They suffered, too, because they knew that some day they must die.

Besides all this suffering, they wanted many things which they thought would make them happier. But very often these things were not what they had known in Paradise to be beautiful, good and true. And when they had them, they suffered still more.

This part of the story tells what happened to our first parents when they did not obey God. Tell the story.

PAGE 9

Original Sin

PAGE 10

III

When our first parents gave to God their love and their obedience, God was pleased with them.

And they had God's blessing for themselves and for their children.

They were happy and their children would be happy too.

But when our first parents did not give to God their love and their obedience, they were very unhappy.

For then they did not have God's blessing.

ADAM WAS THE HEAD OF THE FAMILY. And he had lost God's blessing for his children as well as for himself.

So since that time, children do not have God's Love and Truth in them at the beginning of their lives.

That is why it was that when we were born, we did not have God's Love and Truth in us.

AND THE WORDS "ORIGINAL SIN" mean that we did not have God's Love and Truth in us at the beginning of our lives.

You have learned that after our first parents had disobeyed God, and were no longer holy, they had to suffer death. This suffering comes also to their children. For

PAGE 11

PAGE 12

all children of Adam and Eve must suffer death. And most of their children must suffer from sickness, hard work, heat or cold.

All of them suffer also because they want many things which they think would make them happier. But very often the things they want are not, for them, beautiful, good and true.

And like our first parents, when they have these things, they suffer still more.

This part of the story tells some of the ways Adam's children suffered because he,
THE HEAD OF THE FAMILY,
DISOBEYED GOD.

Tell the story.

I

A PROMISE BY THE GOD OF TRUTH

THE STORIES in **Book One** told us that God is All-Good, that He is doing good things for us all the time, and that the very best thing He does for us is to give us of His Love.

Now, you have read our first parents' sad story. So you know why it was that everything was changed for them. And you know why it was that they were so unhappy.

No matter how hard they tried, they did not have the power to bring back the gift of having God's Love and

"A Child Is Born to Us"

Truth in them. They knew they never would have this power.

AND THIS ONE THING WAS THE SADDEST OF ALL.

But God had pity on our first parents. And He was very, very good to them.

II

You see, God did not want our first parents and you and me ever to forget that He is All-Good. So God did something which took away some of the sadness.

GOD MADE A PROMISE.

And all those who believed this Promise and tried to be true to God, had His blessing.

III

God's Promise was that some day
A CHILD WOULD BE BORN
Who would have greater power than any other child, or any man or woman who would ever live upon this earth.

A very holy man whom God let know many of His secrets once told us something about This Child.

This is what he said:

> "**A Child is born to us**
> **...and His Name**
> **Shall Be Called**
> **Wonderful...**
> **THE PRINCE OF PEACE.**"

PAGE 15

"The Prince of Peace"

For He Would Love Us

The holy man spoke these words because he knew that

THIS ONE CHILD

even when He was a little baby WOULD HAVE THE POWER TO OFFER TO GOD more than enough LOVE AND OBEDIENCE to make up for the turning away from God of our first parents and those who would come after them.

And when He grew to be a man, He would not be afraid to keep on offering His great love and obedience for us, even when He knew that this would mean for Him suffering and death. For He would love us.

HE WOULD DIE FOR US.

PAGE 17

He Would Die for Us

And he would find a way for all children of Adam and Eve TO HAVE GOD'S LOVE AND TRUTH IN THEM.

🕊 🕊 🕊 🕊

As you go on reading the stories in "A Little Child's First Communion," you will learn WHO HAD THE POWER to give God so much love and obedience and WHO WAS ABLE TO FIND A WAY for all children of Adam and Eve to have God's Love and Truth in them.

Ask your father or mother to write your name in the blank space and to sign the page if you can answer all the questions in this test correctly.

A Can - You - Tell Test

Do not answer these questions by only Yes or No.

Tell some sentences from the book which will answer each question.

Can you tell why a boy or girl should want to be truthful?

Can you tell what God wants all of His children to have and to keep in them?

Can you tell what Tom did because he wanted his mother to be happy?

Can you tell why our first parents were happy in Paradise?

Can you tell what they did one sad day?

Can you tell how everything was changed for them and their children?

Can you tell what God did for our first parents which took away some of their sadness?

Can you tell what the words ORIGINAL SIN mean?

Can you tell what the story says about One Child?

.... can answer all the questions in this test correctly.

....
Parent's Signature

GREAT AND HOLY MEN

WHEN Adam and Eve had been dead for about a thousand years, there were many people living upon the earth.

And many of these people did wrong and wicked things. For they did not pay attention to God. And they did not have God's Love and Truth in them.

But God wanted people to pay attention to Him. And He wanted them to have and to keep His Love and Truth in them.

So from time to time God chose a few brave men. And He made them great and holy.

These great and holy men bravely told the people not to be so wicked.

And they tried to make the people understand that they must do what God wanted them to do or they would never have God's blessing.

But most of the people would not pay attention to these great and holy men sent by God.

Tell this story to some one at home.

✯ ✯ ✯ ✯

A Test

Why did the people who would not pay attention to God do many wrong and wicked things?

What did God do to help the people to pay attention to Him once more?

What did God's great and holy men tell the people?

What did most of the people think about these holy men?

PAGE 20

THE GREATEST OF GOD'S HOLY MEN

THERE were many of these great and holy men sent by God, but John was the greatest of them all.

He lived for a long time in a desert.

Honey from wild bees and other things that he found in the desert were his only food. And his clothing was made of the skins of animals.

John was filled with God's Love and Truth, and after a while he began to teach the people.

He told them to be sorry for the bad things they had done. And he said that they should try to do good to poor people as often as they could.

PAGE 22

Most of the men and women coming to listen to John thought that he must be the greatest and holiest teacher whom God would ever send to live upon this earth.

So they were much surprised when John told them that he was not the greatest and holiest teacher. For he said that **God's Own Son was living upon the earth,** and that He would soon begin to teach.

He would be The Greatest and Holiest Teacher. And through His Power, God's Love and Truth would be given to the people.

The king of the country where John was teaching did not believe in God. So he did not love Him. The king was a very

PAGE 23

John Was not Afraid to Die

bad man. And John told him that some of the deeds that he was doing were very wicked. Then the king was angry and told the soldiers to take John to prison.

A wicked woman who was living in the king's palace at that time wanted John put to death so that he could not tell the truth any more.

The king knew that John was good. But to please the wicked woman, he ordered the soldiers to cut off John's head.

John was not afraid to die. For all his life he had loved God's Truth and had done what God wanted him to do.

This John is called Saint John the Baptist.

He was a Saint because he was filled with God's Love and Truth.

He is called the Baptist because he baptized those people who believed what he told them about the coming of God's Own Son, and were sorry for the bad things they had done.

A Test

1. What did Saint John the Baptist tell the people when they came to him in the desert?
2. The people coming to John in the desert thought that he was another person. Who did they think he was?
3. Who did Saint John the Baptist say would begin to teach the people very soon?
4. Saint John was not afraid to die. Why?
5. Why was Saint John the Baptist called a "Saint"?

A STORY ABOUT GOD'S OWN SON

GOD'S Own Son was THE GREATEST AND THE HOLIEST TEACHER the world would ever have.

But until He was thirty years old, He did not go from place to place teaching the people.

When He was thirty years old, He went one day to the river Jordan where Saint John the Baptist was teaching and baptizing many people.

Saint John saw The Son of God among the people to be baptized.

AND HE KNEW WHO HE WAS!

Of course Saint John did not want to baptize The Son of God, and he said:

"A Voice from the Clouds"

"I ought to be baptized by Thee, and comest Thou to me?"

But God's Own Son told Saint John to baptize Him just as he did the other people.

Saint John did as he was told to do.

And then, what do you think happened?

A Voice from the clouds was heard saying:

"THIS IS MY BELOVED SON IN WHOM I AM WELL PLEASED."

You see God wanted all the world to know that **His Own Beloved Son came to live upon this earth.**

And He wanted all the world to know

that **His Own Beloved Son was the God-Man.**

For then everyone COULD ALWAYS BE SURE that He was The One sent to be The Great, True Teacher of us all,

AND THE ONE

Who had the power to offer to His Father such great love and obedience **that He would more than make up for the turning away from God of our first parents** and all those who would come after them.

For they would know THAT HE WOULD KEEP ON offering to His Father great, great love and obedience EVEN WHEN THIS WOULD MEAN

PAGE 27

"Art Thou the Christ?"

FOR HIM SUFFERING AND DEATH.

After God's Own Son had left the river Jordan, He went to different places and taught the people the truth about THE ONE TRUE GOD. For to teach Truth is one reason why He came to live in this world.

But many wicked men hated Him because He was teaching God's Truth and because He let them know that many of the things they were doing were very bad.

And one day a great and wicked leader of the people asked Him this question:

"ART THOU THE CHRIST, THE SON OF THE BLESSED GOD?"

He knew that the wicked men wanted

to kill Him. And He knew that they would kill Him if He told them the truth and said that He was the Son of God.

BUT HE ANSWERED: "I AM."

For His Father wanted all people until the end of the world TO BE SURE that He was His Own Beloved Son.

And He, too, wanted all people to be sure that He was God's Own Beloved Son. **For He wanted them always to know that His teachings are True.**

🙟 🙟 🙟 🙟

God's Own Son was called Jesus. And **Book Three** will tell more about Jesus.

PAGE 30

GOD'S OWN SON

Music by
CORNELIA S. CRANE

God sent His own Be-lov-ed Son, To teach the world and show the way Of goodness, beauty and of truth; O let us learn of Him to-day.

A Test: Who?

WHO SAID THE WORDS?

"Art thou the Christ, the Son of the blessed God?"

"I Am."

"This is My Beloved Son in Whom I am well pleased."

"I ought to be baptized by Thee, and comest Thou to me?"

WHO DID THE DEED?

God's Own Son went one day to the river Jordan where He was baptized.

They were cruel to Him because they hated Him.

After He left the river Jordan, He went to different places and taught the people.

WHO WAS THE PERSON?

The greatest and holiest of all teachers.

He wanted people until the end of the world to know that His teachings are true.

He let the people know that The One Who had just been baptized was His Own Son.

To teach Truth is one reason why He came to live in this world.

.... has studied Book Two and has done this test correctly.

....
Parent's Signature

PAGE 31

PAGE 32

Ask your father or mother to write your name in the blank spaces and to sign this page.

.... has done correctly the tests on pages 4, 18, 20, 24.

.... can say or sing the verse on page 5.

.... can say or sing the verse on page 30.

.... can tell in a child's own words what this book teaches about the greatest of God's holy men.

.... can tell in a child's own words what this book teaches about God's Own Son.

.... has done neatly the following project work:

1. Draw or paste a picture of **Tom praying.** Write a sentence telling what Tom was asking God.

2. Children of Adam and Eve suffer from hard work, heat, cold, sickness and death. Paste one or more pictures showing that this sentence is true. Under the pictures, write sentences telling why all this suffering came into the world.

3. Paste a picture showing God's Own Son teaching the people.

Under the picture, write some sentences which tell what the picture teaches us.

....
Parent's Signature

BOOK THREE
STORIES ABOUT JESUS

The stories in *Book Two* told you about The God of Truth and His Promise to our first parents. They also told you the reason why God's Own Beloved Son came to live upon this earth.

And now would you like to know about
GOD'S OWN BELOVED SON AS A LITTLE BABY?

Would you like to know more about His life
WHEN HE GREW TO BE A MAN?

And would you like to know what He did
TO PROVE THAT HE IS GOD?

The stories in Book Three will tell you
THE ANSWERS TO THESE QUESTIONS.

Approved by the National Center of the Confraternity of Christian Doctrine

JESUS' MOTHER

NE of the best gifts that God gives to every child is a mother. And God wanted His Own Son to have a lovely Mother.

The name of the one whom God wanted to be the Mother of His Own Son was Mary. And God sent a messenger TO TELL THE LOVELY, HOLY MARY THAT HE WANTED HER TO BE THE MOTHER OF HIS OWN SON.

The messenger also told Mary that God wanted His Own Son called JESUS.

The messenger was a bright and beautiful angel.

We do not see angels. But God let Mary

see the angel who brought His message to her.

From the angel's message Mary knew that God wanted His Own Beloved Son to come to earth as a little Baby and to live upon the earth as other people live.

Mary was sure that if God's Own Son came to this earth as one of us, He would offer to His Father, for us,

GREAT LOVE AND OBEDIENCE.

He would more than make up for the failure in love and obedience of Adam and all the other people belonging to Adam's family, from the beginning to the end of the world.

She was sure, too, that God's Own

PAGE 3

Son would leave a SURE WAY, "A HOLY WAY," "A STRAIGHT WAY" for all people to have God's Love and Truth in them.

And she remembered what the holy man had said about ONE CHILD Who would some time be born and Who would be "THE PRINCE OF PEACE" and "WONDERFUL."

From the very beginning of her life, Mary was filled with God's Love and Truth.

She always wanted whatever was most pleasing to God. And she made the angel understand that, if God wanted it, she was happy to be the Mother of His Own Son.

The Story Told by a Daisy

Draw a daisy with six petals on a piece of heavy white paper.

Color the center of the daisy yellow.

Cut out the daisy.

Write the answer to each question on one of the white petals.

When you have finished, ask someone at home if the answers are right.

Then paste the daisy in your notebook or put it in your room near the statue of Jesus' Mother.

✼ ✼ ✼

1. Write a word that tells about the Mother of God's Own Son.

2. Write the name of The Mother of God's Own Son.

3. What did God give Mary at the very beginning of her life?

4. What Name was given to God's Own Son?

5. Who are God's messengers?

6. Write two words telling what God's Own Son would offer to His Father.

THE MOTHER OF JESUS

Music by
CORNELIA S. CRANE

God's Son had a love-ly Mo-ther Fill'd with His beau-ty was she; O, Mo-ther of God, please help us to grow ve-ry love-ly like thee.

THE STORY OF SAINT JOSEPH

SAINT JOSEPH was a carpenter.

He was very holy. For God had given Saint Joseph of His Love and Truth.

When God's Own Son was coming to live upon this earth, God wanted SOMETHING IMPORTANT done for Him. He chose Saint Joseph to do this. And He sent an angel with His message.

The angel let Saint Joseph know that GOD'S OWN SON would soon be living upon this earth as we do.

The angel also let Saint Joseph know that God wanted him to take care of His Own Son, and of Mary whom God had chosen to be The Mother of His Own Son.

PAGE 6

THE ANGEL'S MESSAGE MADE SAINT JOSEPH VERY, VERY HAPPY.

Fill each space with a word that makes a true story.

Write the stories in your First Communion Notebook.

1. Saint Joseph was a ....

2. God gave Saint Joseph of His .... and ....

3. God chose .... to do something important for Him.

4. God sent Saint Joseph a message by an ....

5. The angel let Saint Joseph know that .... would soon be living upon this earth.

6. God wanted Saint Joseph to take care of ....

✓ ✓ ✓

Project Work

Find a picture of Saint Joseph. Paste this picture in your First Communion Notebook or on a project page. Under the picture write some sentences about Saint Joseph.

PAGE 7

Saint
Joseph
Was
Very
Happy

PRAYER

When we pray we talk to someone.

We show that we love this one.

We ask this one to help us.

Here is a prayer which you should say every morning and every evening — to talk to The Mother of God's Own Son, to show her that you love her, and to ask her to pray for you.

The Hail Mary

HAIL MARY, full of grace, the Lord is with thee; blessed art thou among women, and blessed is the fruit of thy womb, Jesus.

Holy Mary, Mother of God, pray for us sinners now and at the hour of our death. Amen.

Project Work

Find some pictures of Jesus' Mother.

Paste them in your First Communion Notebook or on project pages. And under the pictures write some sentences telling about Jesus' Mother.

THE STORY OF THE BABY JESUS

MARY knew from the angel's message that God's Own Son was coming to this earth as a little Baby.

AND GOD'S OWN SON DID COME TO THIS EARTH AS A LITTLE BABY.

His birthday is called CHRISTMAS.

He did not come to a rich and beautiful home. He came to a cave which was used as a stable for animals.

And this is the story of His coming.

The Roman governor was making a list of all the people in the country. And Mary and Joseph had come to Bethlehem

PAGE 10

to have their names written on the governor's list.

As many other people had come to Bethlehem, there was not a house in the town where Mary could stay for the night.

This cave was the only place Joseph could find for her.

And at night when the cave was very dark and still, God's Own Son came to this earth. Then the singing of angels was heard and the cave became bright and beautiful.

Mary and Joseph both knew that The Baby was God's Own Son.

And they knew that the whole

world would be different because this little Baby had come to live in it.

They knew that He had come to give God's Love and Truth to the whole world.

They knelt upon the floor of the cave.

They were the very first to give The Baby Jesus their love.

🌱 🌱 🌱 🌱

Prayer to the Baby Jesus

DEAR *Baby Jesus, I will shut my eyes and make believe that I am kneeling on the floor of the cave with Mary and Joseph. For I wish that I could have been there that night to give You my love.*

Tell the story of The Baby Jesus to some other children.

MAKING SACRIFICES

The Baby Jesus had very few things. He was poor.

We shall be more like The Baby Jesus if we do not want too many things.

So, at times we can go without something we like very much, just to show that we want to be more like The One Who loved us so much.

When we do this, we make a sacrifice.

Perhaps you would like to make these sacrifices or some others:

. . . **You can go without some of your play to do something which you think would please your mother.**

. . . **When you feel like being cross, you can say or do something kind.**

. . . **When you feel like eating more cake or candy or something else that you like, you can refuse to take it when it is passed to you.**

Paste a picture of The Baby Jesus in your First Communion Notebook or on a project page. Under it write the prayer on page 11.

PAGE 12

THE BABY JESUS

Music by
CORNELIA S. CRANE

Hail to Thee lit-tle Ba-by Je-sus, Thou who art the Son of God, To the crib with Ma-ry and Jos-eph, To of-fer Thee love I come

Child's Name

....

— can tell in a child's own words what this book teaches about The Mother of Jesus.

— can tell "The Story of Saint Joseph."

— can tell what God did to let Mary know that He wanted her to be the Mother of His Own Son.

— has done correctly the tests on pages 4 and 7.

— knows what the book teaches on page 8 about prayer.

— has said the "Hail Mary" every morning and evening.

— has told the story of The Baby Jesus to some other children.

— knows what the birthday of God's Own Son is called.

— knows where The Baby Jesus was born.

— knows what The Baby Jesus came to give to the people.

— knows what the book tells about sacrifices.

— can say or sing the verse "The Baby Jesus."

— knows the "Prayer to The Baby Jesus."

— can say or sing the verse "God's Own Son." It is in *Book Two*.

— knows Acts of Faith, Hope and Love (see *Book One*).

— can say or sing the verse "The Mother of Jesus."

PAGE 14

....

Parent's Signature

PAGE 15

THE BABY JESUS' VISITORS

"WHILE all things were in quiet silence," Jesus was born.

Some shepherds were keeping the night watch over their flocks near Bethlehem. Angels let them know that God's Own Son had come to live upon this earth. Then they left their sheep and came hurrying across the hills to the cave. They knelt and gave The Baby Jesus their love.

Then they went back to take care of their sheep and told all the people they met that **God's Own Son had come to earth.**

The Baby Jesus had visitors from far away as well as from Bethlehem.

Some wise men, called Magi, who liked

to study the stars, lived a long way from Bethlehem. One night they saw a new star in the sky. This star was brighter than the other stars and different from any star that they had ever seen.

These wise men had heard that God's Own Son would come some day to live upon this earth. When they saw this bright new star, they were sure that the time had come.

Three of these men started out on the long journey across the desert to find the place where God's Own Son was living. They rode on camels.

The bright new star moved in the sky and showed them the way. But when they came to Jerusalem, they could not

PAGE 16

see the star, so they asked King Herod if he could tell them the way to go.

Before they left the king, they learned that The One for Whom they had come across the desert was living in Bethlehem. And when they started toward Bethlehem, they saw the star again. It went before them until it came to the place where The Baby Jesus was.

"And entering into the house," they knelt and gave The Baby Jesus their love.

They also gave Him beautiful gifts which they had brought with them from their own country.

Tell this story to some other children.

PAGE 17

THE HOLY FAMILY

WE CALL Jesus, Mary and Joseph **The Holy Family.**

After the Magi had visited the Holy Family and were on their way back to their own country, God sent an angel to let Saint Joseph know that the wicked King Herod would try to kill The Baby Jesus. Then during the night Saint Joseph took The Child and His Mother out of their own country into another country called Egypt.

This cruel king wanted to kill The Baby Jesus because he was afraid that when The Baby Jesus was older, the people would make Him their King.

But Herod wanted to keep on being

PAGE 19

king until the end of his life. After that, he wanted his son to be king. So he had the soldiers kill many children, hoping that one of them might be The Baby Jesus.

The Holy Family lived in Egypt until Saint Joseph knew that it would be safe to bring The Baby Jesus back to His Own country.

Tell someone at home why The Holy Family hurried into Egypt.

🙟 🙟 🙟 🙟

THE STORY OF JESUS' LIFE

WHEN The Holy Family left Egypt and came back into their own country, they lived for many years in a little village called Nazareth.

PAGE 20

And Jesus made Mary and Joseph very happy by His obedience and love.

At that time only a few people knew that Jesus was The Son of God.

But when Jesus was thirty years old, He went from place to place teaching the people about The One True God.

And He let them know that He was God's Own Son.

Fathers and mothers brought their children to Him so that He would bless them.

And many people followed Him from place to place, because they wanted to hear more and more of God's Truth, and also because He did many good things for them. He made sick people well. He even made some people who were dead come back to life.

JESUS TAUGHT TRUTH AND HE DID EVERYTHING WITH LOVE.

For He was God's Own Son. And you know that God is All-Truth and All-Love.

🌱 🌱 🌱 🌱

"A STORY about God's Own Son," which you read in **Book Two,** told you that wicked men wanted Jesus put to death so that He could not teach the people the truth any more.

These wicked men were very cruel to

PAGE 21

JESUS'
CRUEL
DEATH

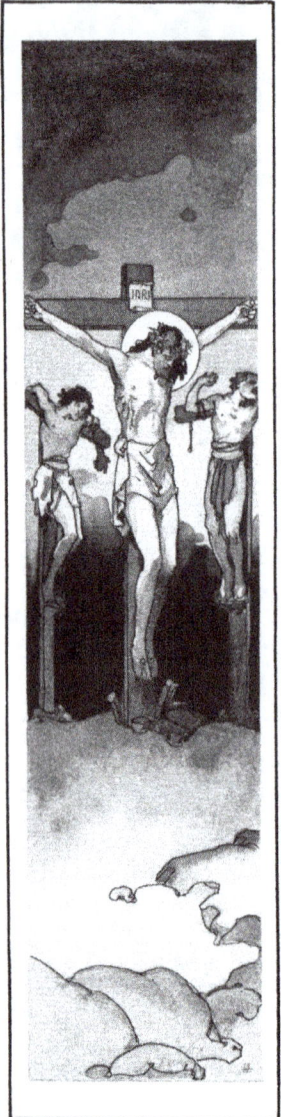

PAGE 22

Jesus and at last they made Him carry a big, heavy cross and nailed Him to it.

Jesus' Mother, Mary, stood by The Cross until Jesus died.

Two thieves were dying on crosses near Jesus.

After a while one thief believed that Jesus was God's Own Son. And when this thief looked at Jesus, he was sorry for the bad things he had done.

He spoke to Jesus and said:

"Lord, remember me when Thou shalt come into Thy kingdom."

Then Jesus promised the thief that He would take him to be happy with Him forever in HEAVEN.

For HEAVEN is the name of Jesus' kingdom.

In the story, "The First Man and Woman," which you read in **Book Two,** you learned that our first parents did not give to God the love and obedience they knew they should give to Him.

They turned away from God.

The story, "God's Promise," which is also in **Book Two,** told you about GOD'S GREAT PROMISE. And you will remember that God's Great Promise was that He would send Someone to live upon this earth Who would give Him GREATER love and obedience than anyone else could give.

PAGE 23

Jesus' Mother, Mary, Stood by the Cross

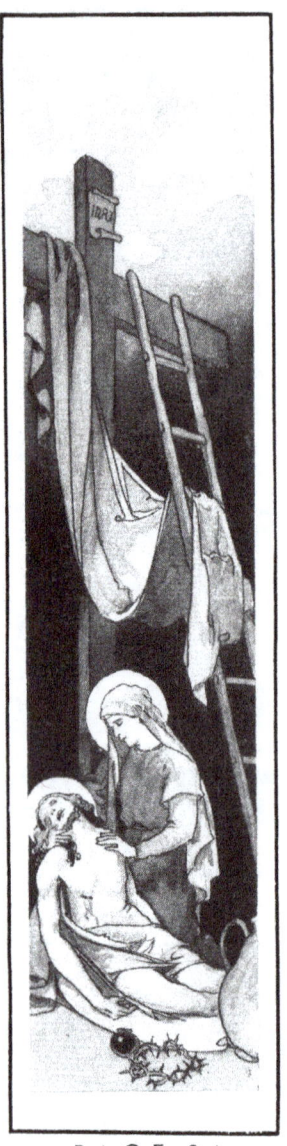

PAGE 24

Now you know from several stories that Jesus, God's Own Beloved Son, offered to His Father, love and obedience, "EVEN TO THE DEATH OF THE CROSS."

For Jesus lived and suffered and died to give to His Father so much love and obedience that He would more than make up

FOR THE FAILURE

in love and obedience of Adam and all the other people belonging to Adam's family from the beginning to the end of the world.

All the other people who ever had lived or ever would live in the world could not give to God as much love and obedience as Jesus gave.

PAGE 25

For we must always remember that Jesus was God's Own Beloved Son.

And Jesus wanted all of us to be His Father's very dear children.

For He wanted all of us to do as He did and offer to His Father ALL THE LOVE AND OBEDIENCE in our power.

Jesus Offered Great Love and Obedience

🌱 🌱 🌱 🌱

Book Four will tell you about the sure way, "the holy way," "the straight way" that Jesus left so that we may have God's Love and Truth in us.

THE PRAYER WHICH JESUS TAUGHT US

One day Jesus' friends saw Him praying. When Jesus' prayer was finished, one of them said to Him:

"Lord, teach us to pray."

Then Jesus taught them this prayer:

The Lord's Prayer

Our Father who art in heaven,
Hallowed be Thy Name,
Thy kingdom come,
Thy will be done on earth, as it is in heaven.
Give us this day our daily bread;
And forgive us our trespasses, as we forgive
Those who trespass against us,
And lead us not into temptation,
But deliver us from evil.
Amen.

Ask your father or mother to hear you say this prayer every morning and evening.

A Test

PAGE 27

Parts of sentences are given in each list. Put the right parts of the sentences together. Write them in your First Communion Notebook or on a project page. Ask someone at home to see if your sentences are right.

LIST ONE

When Jesus was a boy He lived at Nazareth, ...

When Jesus was thirty years old ....

Jesus was ....

Jesus died ....

Jesus' Mother stood by the Cross ....

The name of Jesus' kingdom ....

LIST TWO

.... He went from place to place teaching the people.

.... until Jesus died.

.... is heaven.

.... nailed to a Cross.

.... obeying His Mother Mary and Saint Joseph.

.... God's Own Son.

A STORY SHOWING THAT JESUS IS GOD

THE people could see that Jesus was a man.

But some did not believe that He was also God.

So Jesus proved to the people that He was God.

For HE ROSE FROM THE DEAD.

And no one but Jesus had the power to rise from the dead.

Jesus died on a Friday.

He was put in a tomb. A big stone was rolled against the door. Soldiers stood outside. They were left there to watch the tomb and to be sure that no one moved the stone.

PAGE 28

But on Sunday morning, when Jesus' friends came to visit the tomb, they saw that the stone had been rolled back!

The soldiers were not there!

So Jesus' friends went into the tomb.

They were looking for the Body of Jesus.

But they did not find the Body of Jesus!

They were surprised, and wondered where Jesus' Body could be.

And, behold! They saw two shining angels standing near them.

They bowed very low.

Then they heard the angels saying:

PAGE 29

"Remember How He Spoke unto You"

"He is not here, but risen,

Remember how He spoke unto you . . .

Saying:

The Son of Man must be . . . crucified

And the third day rise again."

✦ ✦ ✦

Then Jesus' friends remembered that Jesus HAD TOLD the people that He would rise from the dead.

The angels' message filled them with great joy.

And they went quickly away to tell Jesus' other friends what had happened.

PAGE 31

THEY WATCHED JESUS ASCEND INTO HEAVEN

AFTER Jesus had risen from the dead, many of His friends saw Him and talked with Him.

Jesus stayed upon this earth forty days.

He did not die again.

But one day while His friends were with Him, He told them that He was going to leave them to go back to His Father in heaven.

Then, they saw Him, RISING BY HIS OWN POWER.

And they watched Him until the clouds hid Him from their sight.

PAGE 32

Tell someone at home the story of how Jesus rose from the dead and stayed forty days upon this earth. And ask someone at home to tell you the names given to:

the day Jesus died,

the day Jesus rose from the dead,

the day Jesus went back to His Father in heaven.

Can you answer these questions?

1. What did Jesus' friends say to Him one day when they saw Him praying?
2. On what day did Jesus die?
3. After Jesus was dead, where was His Body laid?
4. Who watched outside of Jesus' tomb?
5. On what day did Jesus rise from the dead?
6. How do we know that Jesus rose from the dead?
7. On what day did Jesus go back to His Father in heaven?

Project Work

1. Draw seven circles in your First Communion Notebook or on project pages. Color the circles. Or cut from paper seven circles of different colors.

Write the answer to each of the seven questions in a circle.

2. Find a picture of Jesus on the Cross, a picture of Jesus after He had risen from the dead, and a picture of Jesus going back to His Father in heaven. Paste these pictures in your First Communion Notebook or on project pages. Write, under each picture, what the picture shows.

A Play

What to use for the play:

Which door of this room shall we call the door of the tomb?

What shall we use for the big stone?

What can the soldiers carry for swords?

How shall we know the angel?

What to do:

Act 1

The Soldiers:

Watch the tomb.

See the stone rolled away by an angel.

Run away frightened.

Jesus' Friends:

Hurry to the tomb.

Show surprise.

Look sad because The Body of Jesus is not there.

Act 2

The Angels:

Speak to Jesus' friends as the angels do in the story.

Jesus' Friends:

Listen to the angels.

Show great joy.

One friend tells the others that Jesus did say that He would rise from the dead.

All hurry away to tell the others the joyous news.

PAGE 34

PROTECT ME BY THY POWER

Music by
CORNELIA S. CRANE

Since Thou didst rise up from the dead, Je-sus, Thou art God, I know; Then I need nev-er be a-fraid, For Thou wilt guard me as I go.

Child's Name

....

— has told the story about The Baby Jesus' visitors to some other children or to someone at home.

— knows what the shepherds told the people after they had visited The Baby Jesus.

— knows what "the wise men" are called.

— knows how "the wise men" found the way to Bethlehem.

— knows what the Magi did when they came to Jerusalem; what they did when they found The Baby Jesus.

— says "The Lord's Prayer" and the "Hail Mary" every morning and evening.

— can do the tests on pages 27 and 32.

— knows what Jesus taught the people when He went to different places.

— knows the story of Jesus' Life and cruel Death.

— knows what Jesus promised the thief who was sorry for his sins.

— knows to Whom we are talking when we say "The Lord's Prayer."

— knows how Jesus proved to the people that He was God.

— knows on what day Jesus died.

— knows on what day Jesus rose from the dead.

— has acted, with some other children, the play on page 33.

— can sing or say the verse "Protect Me by Thy Power."

— has kept a neat First Communion Notebook or has finished some neat project pages approved by the teacher.

....
Parent's Signature

PAGE 35

A STORY ABOUT THE HOLY GHOST

BEFORE Jesus left this earth and went back to His Father,

He promised those who followed Him that He would send The Holy Ghost.

And Jesus did send The Holy Ghost. But The Holy Ghost never lived upon this earth as Jesus did.

We do not see The Holy Ghost. But The Holy Ghost will keep on giving people God's Love until the end of the world.

And The Holy Ghost will keep on "teaching all truth" until the end of the world.

PAGE 36

"The Father is God; The Son is God; The Holy Ghost is God; and yet they are not three gods but one God."

IN GOD THERE ARE THREE PERSONS;

The Father,
The Son,
and
The Holy Ghost

WE CALL THE THREE PERSONS IN ONE GOD THE HOLY TRINITY.

PAGE 37

"There Are Not Three Gods but One God"

PAGE 38

A PRAYER TO THE HOLY GHOST
Music by
CORNELIA S. CRANE

O Holy Ghost, come Thou to me;
Teach me to know the truth I pray;
Grant me wherever I may be, To
grow in love of Thee each day.

A Test

Finish these sentences by putting the right words in the blank spaces.

Jesus promised that when He went back to His Father He would send The ....

The Holy Ghost is ....

The .... never lived upon this earth as Jesus did.

When The Holy Ghost is with us He teaches us ....

When The Holy Ghost is with us He gives us more and more of God's ....

The Father is ....; The Son is ....; .... is God; and yet They are .... three gods but .... God.

In One God there are Three Persons:
    The Father,
    The Son and
    The ....

We call the Three Persons in one God, ...

Write these sentences in your First Communion Notebook or on a project page. Ask someone at home to tell you if your sentences are right.

PAGE 39

PAGE 40

 A SALUTE to The Father, The Son and The Holy Ghost

Catholic children at school salute the flag of their country every day.

But they love to salute The Holy Trinity, Father, Son and Holy Ghost, several times each day.

They do this by making *The Sign of the Cross.*

Be sure that you know how to make The Sign of the Cross correctly.

 **1** First, place your left hand on your breast.  **2** Then, touch your forehead with your right hand saying:

"IN THE NAME OF THE FATHER";

 **3** Lower the right hand and touch the breast saying:

"AND OF THE SON";

 **4** Then touch the left shoulder and  **5** next the right shoulder, at the same time saying:

"AND OF THE HOLY GHOST."

 **6** Join your hands together and say:

"AMEN."

PAGE 41

STORIES TELLING HOW TO BE LIKE JESUS

J ESUS is our Model.

The more we have of God's Love and Truth in us, the more like Jesus we become. And as we become more like Jesus, we act more like Him. This means that we give to Our Heavenly Father more and more love and obedience.

These stories tell many things that Jesus did. If you study them, they will help you to know our Model better.

🙢 🙢 🙢

1 Jesus knew when the time had come for the wicked men to take Him prisoner and put Him to death. Then Jesus prayed

with great love to His Father for many hours.

And many times when Jesus was getting ready to do a very big work, He spent a long time praying to His Father with love.

Read the sentence below, filling in the blank spaces:

You will be like Jesus in one way if you .... to God often and with much ....

🙢

2 Jesus loved His Father and His Father's goodness very much more than the whole world and all the people and things in it.

Jesus Was All-Holy

And Jesus always did good deeds.

Jesus was All-Holy.

And Jesus wants us to be holy.

Read the sentence below, filling in the blank spaces:
You will be holy if you love .... and His goodness most of all, and if you always do .... deeds.

✻ ✻ ✻

3 Jesus went from place to place teaching the people the truth about God.

And He did everything with love.

He made the sick well.

He made the blind see.

He showed love to everyone, to those who were good to Him and to those who were not good to Him.

"I Am The Truth"

Read the sentence below, filling in the blank spaces:

You will be like Jesus in one way if you show .... to everyone, to those who are .... to you, and to those who are not .... to you.

⁘

4 Jesus said: "I am the Truth." And Jesus taught that everyone who loves the truth pays attention to His words.

Read the sentences below, filling in the blank spaces:

Jesus said: "I am the ...."

You will be like Jesus in one way if you always love the ....

⁘

5 In His home at Nazareth Jesus was obedient to His Mother Mary and to Saint Joseph.

PAGE 44

PAGE 45

And Jesus obeyed the laws of His country. But, above all, Jesus always obeyed all of His Father's laws.

Read the sentence below, filling in the blank space:

You will be like Jesus in one way if you .... your father and mother, and others whom you know you should obey.

✿ ✿ ✿

6 When those who were going from place to place with Jesus wanted to send away the little children, Jesus was kind and gentle and asked them to let the little children come to Him.

One day when Jesus saw a mother crying because her only son was dead, Jesus showed that He was kind and gentle. He

Jesus Did Everything with Love

said: "Weep not." And then He brought her son to life again.

Read the sentence below, filling in the blank spaces:

You will be like Jesus in one way if you are .... and .... with everyone.

☙ ☙ ☙

[7] Jesus, God's Own Son, showed by the place in which He was born, and by the way He lived, that He did not want the things that other people want so much. So He taught us that we can be good and happy even if we do not have all the things that we want.

Read the sentence below, filling in the blank spaces:

You will be like .... in one way, if you are never sad because another person has something which

PAGE 46

PAGE 47

you cannot have; and if .... never do anything unfair to that person who has .... which you do not have.

🌱 🌱 🌱

<u>8</u> Jesus had the power to offer to His Father more love and obedience than anyone else could offer to Him.

Read the sentence below, filling in the blank spaces:

You will be .... Jesus in one way if you offer to God all the .... and obedience which you are able to give Him.

🌱 🌱 🌱

Ask your mother or your teacher to tell you some other ways that you can be like Jesus, Who is our Model.

In your First Communion Notebook or on project pages paste some pictures of Jesus, our Model. Under each picture write one or more sentences telling what the picture teaches.

JESUS' COMMANDMENTS OF LOVE

You will act like Jesus in all the ways told in the stories which you have just read if you obey Jesus' two Great Commandments of Love.

Jesus' **First** Great Commandment of Love

In the greatest of Jesus' Commandments He tells us that we should FIRST OF ALL

LOVE GOD
WITH OUR WHOLE STRENGTH.

And this means that we should love God more than anyone or anything else.

Jesus' **Second** Great Commandment of Love

Jesus tells us that we should love all people — those who are good to us and those who are not good to us. For at the very same time that He gave us His First Great Commandment, He also gave us the Second Great Commandment:

"LOVE THY NEIGHBOR AS THYSELF."

And He said at another time,

"Love One Another As I Have Loved You."

Learn Jesus' great Commandments about loving God and other people.

PAGE 49

Jesus Is Our Great, True Teacher

THE TEN COMMANDMENTS

PAGE 50

LONG before Jesus came to this earth, God gave TEN COMMANDMENTS to His people. You may learn more about these Commandments later. But if you try to be like Jesus as the stories tell you, ALWAYS REMEMBERING His Great Commandments of Love, you will do all that God expects of you now.

The Ten Commandments are:

1. I am the Lord thy God. Thou shalt not have strange gods before Me.
2. Thou shalt not take the name of the Lord thy God in vain.
3. Remember thou keep holy the Sabbath Day.
4. Honor thy father and thy mother.
5. Thou shalt not kill.
6. Thou shalt not commit adultery.
7. Thou shalt not steal.
8. Thou shalt not bear false witness against thy neighbor.
9. Thou shalt not covet thy neighbor's wife.
10. Thou shalt not covet thy neighbor's goods.

Child's Name

PAGE 51

....

— has done correctly the tests on pages 39, 41-47.

— can tell in a child's own words what this book teaches about The Holy Ghost.

— can tell all that this book teaches about The Holy Trinity.

— knows how to make The Sign of the Cross correctly.

— knows Jesus' first and greatest Commandment.

— knows Jesus' second great Commandment.

— knows what Jesus' first great Commandment means.

— knows what Jesus' second great Commandment means.

— knows eight ways of being like Jesus.

— knows how many Commandments God had given to the people before Jesus came to give His Commandments of Love.

— says Acts of Faith, Hope and Love every day (see *Book One*).

— can say and write perfectly "The Lord's Prayer" and the "Hail Mary."

— can say or sing the verse, "The Baby Jesus."

— can say or sing the verse, "Protect Me by Thy Power."

— can say or sing "A Prayer to The Holy Ghost."

— has kept a neat First Communion Notebook or has finished some neat project pages approved by the teacher.

....

Parent's Signature

BOOK FOUR

STORIES ABOUT WONDERFUL THINGS THAT JESUS DID FOR US

Before Jesus went back to His Father in heaven
He left us some wonderful gifts.

ONE OF JESUS' GREATEST GIFTS TO US
IS "THE HOLY WAY," "THE STRAIGHT WAY"
He left so that we may always know
GOD'S TRUTH.

And on the night before Jesus died
HE GAVE WONDERFUL POWER
TO HIS PRIESTS.

The stories in Book Four will tell you about
"The Holy Way," "The Straight Way," and
The Wonderful Power Jesus gave to His Priests.

Approved by the National Center of the Confraternity of Christian Doctrine

PAGE 1

WHY GOD SENT HIS OWN BELOVED SON

N Book Two you read that God had pity on our first parents and their children.

And you know that He was very, very good to them.

For you have read about His Promise to send ONE CHILD to earth Who would have greater power than any other child or any man or woman who would ever live upon the earth.

And in **Book Three** you read that
THIS PROMISED CHILD WAS BORN
AND THAT HE WAS
GOD'S OWN BELOVED SON.

God had sent His Own Son to earth to

The Power of the God-Man

be one of us. For He knew that His Own Son loved us with a great love.

He knew that when His Own Son became THE GOD-MAN, He would offer for us His sufferings and His cruel Death with all His great love and obedience.

And He knew that

THE GOD-MAN WOULD BE

for all people

THE GREATEST TEACHER
HOLY AND TRUE,

and that

HE WOULD HAVE THE POWER
TO MAKE ALL PEOPLE HOLY
WITH HIS OWN LOVE AND TRUTH.

PAGE 2

JESUS' OWN WORDS

WE KNOW now that it was Jesus Who was God's Own Beloved Son and THE ONE WHO was sent to the people.

And you have read that while Jesus was living upon this earth He let the people know that He was God's Own Son.

He told them that whatever belonged to The Father was also His and that whenever they asked The Father anything in His Name with great Faith, The Father would give it to them.

So, you see that if we love Jesus and try to be like Him, we are sure that The Father will give us all that we ask in Jesus' Name. But if the gift we ask Him to give us would

bring sorrow instead of joy, our Father, Who loves us, will then give us a better gift.

These are Jesus' own Words:

"All things whatsoever The Father hath ARE MINE.

"Amen, amen, I say to you: if you ask The Father anything in My Name,

"HE WILL GIVE IT (TO) YOU."

"But let him ask in Faith."

Tell what Jesus taught the people about Himself.
Tell what this story teaches about prayer.
Tell Jesus' own words as given in this story.
Tell why God sent His Own Beloved Son to be the people's Teacher.
Tell what God's Own Son could give to the people to make them more like Him and His Father.
Tell what The God-Man could offer for us.

PAGE 4

PAGE 5

WHAT JESUS GAVE TO THE PEOPLE

JESUS filled the hearts of the people with His Own Love and Truth.
He did this
IF THEY WERE SORRY
for the bad things they had done, and
IF THEY BELIEVED
that He was God's Own Son,
sent by The Father
to give them
OF HIS LOVE AND TRUTH.

✶ ✶ ✶

What did Jesus want the people to have in their hearts?
Why did Jesus want the people to be sorry?
What did Jesus want the people to believe?
Who had the power to fill the hearts of the people with God's Love and Truth?

JESUS SPEAKS WITH HIS APOSTLES

WHEN Jesus was speaking with His Apostles one day, He said to them:

"**A little while,** and now you shall not see Me; and **again a little while,** and you shall see Me: because I go to The Father."

When Jesus said these words to His Apostles, He was letting them know
that He would soon die,
after three days rise again,
and after forty days go back to His Father in heaven.

Jesus knew that after He went back to His Father in heaven, the people would no longer be able to see or hear Him.

AND JESUS LOVED US ALL SO VERY, VERY MUCH that He wanted to help us.

What did Jesus say about "a little while"?

What did Jesus let His Apostles know about the time He would die? About His rising again? About His going back to His Father in heaven?

Why did Jesus think that the people would soon feel sad?

JESUS OFFERS LOVE AND OBEDIENCE

JESUS was able to do whatever He wanted to do.

SO JESUS DID FOR US WHAT NO ONE ELSE COULD DO.

While Jesus was living and suffering upon this earth as one of us, He was always

PAGE 8

offering to His Father greater love and obedience than all others could give.

And He knew that when He would be dying upon The Cross, He would keep on offering to His Father THIS SAME GREAT LOVE AND OBEDIENCE.

Adam, the first man and the head of us all, did not give to God, all the love and obedience that he knew he should give to Him. He turned away from God.

But Jesus, God's Own Beloved Son, would offer to His Father so much love and obedience
AND SUFFERING
that He would MORE than make up

PAGE 9

for the disobedience of Adam and Eve and that of their children.

AND JESUS KNEW THAT HIS FATHER WAS WELL PLEASED.

✶ ✶ ✶

Tell what Jesus was always offering to His Father.
Tell what Jesus would keep on offering to His Father even when He was dying upon The Cross.
Tell what the first man failed to give to God.
Tell what Jesus offered to make up for the disobedience of Adam and Eve and that of their children.

✶ ✶ ✶ ✶

B UT Jesus would do still more for the children of Adam and Eve. Before going back to His Father in heaven, He would leave with them until the end of the world

"THE HOLY WAY"

"THE STRAIGHT WAY"

A TRUE TEACHER

and

A SURE WAY

to have GOD'S LOVE AND TRUTH in them.

And Jesus' Church is "THE HOLY WAY," "THE STRAIGHT WAY" Jesus left that we may always KNOW THE TRUTHS that He taught us

ABOUT HIS FATHER,

ABOUT HIMSELF

and ABOUT THE HOLY GHOST.

Tell what we mean by "the holy way," "the straight way."

For how long a time did Jesus want the people to have a True Teacher?

Tell what Jesus' Church will help us to know.

PAGE 10

THE SACRAMENTS

WE CANNOT now see Jesus as those people did who were living at the very same time that Jesus was going from place to place. But we know that Jesus was **teaching** the people of that time, and **filling their hearts** with God's Love and Truth if they believed what He taught them about His Father, about Himself and about The Holy Ghost.

But it is this very same Jesus Who now gives us of God's Love and Truth THROUGH THE SACRAMENTS OF HIS CHURCH.

There are seven Sacraments.

Other lessons in "A Little Child's First

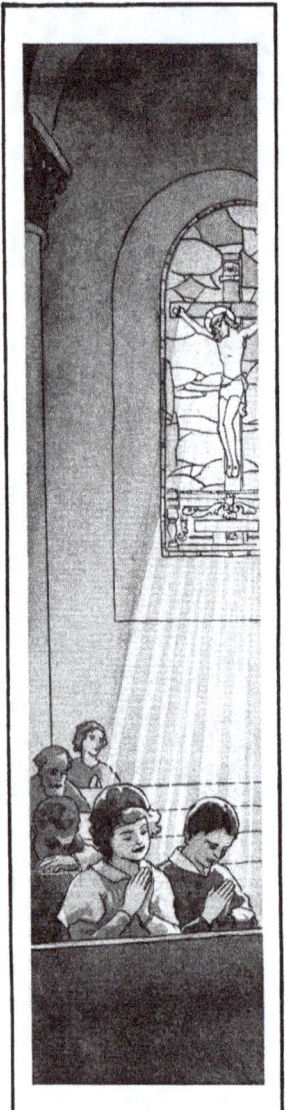

Communion" will tell you the names of these seven Sacraments and something about each one of them.

Another way of saying that we receive GOD'S LOVE AND TRUTH through the Sacraments of Jesus' Church is to say that we receive GOD'S GRACE.

And still another way of saying that we receive GOD'S LOVE AND TRUTH through the Sacraments is to say that we receive THE LIGHT OF GRACE.

⁊ ⁊ ⁊

What did Jesus do for the people when He was living upon this earth?
How does this very same Jesus give us of God's Love and Truth now?
How many Sacraments are there?
Tell two different ways of saying that we receive God's Love and Truth through the Sacraments.

THE HOLY CATHOLIC CHURCH

Everyone who loves Jesus loves THE CHURCH THAT JESUS LEFT to keep on TEACHING GOD'S TRUTH and BRINGING GOD'S GRACE to the world.

AND THE CHURCH

THAT JESUS LEFT

IS

THE HOLY CATHOLIC CHURCH.

✦ ✦ ✦

Why should we all love Jesus' Church?

What is the name of the Church that Jesus left us?

Tell what you can do to show that you love Jesus' Church.

THE FEAST OF PENTECOST

IN **Book Three,** you read that Jesus rose from the dead and stayed forty days upon the earth before He went back to His Father in heaven.

During those forty days, Jesus told His Apostles what He wanted them to do for the people.

He also gave them great power. **For they were to be the first Bishops of His Church.**

And He promised them that when He went back to His Father in heaven, **He would send The Holy Ghost** to be with them always.

So on Sunday, ten days after Jesus had left this earth, when Jesus' Mother, His Apostles and His friends were together in prayer,

THE HOLY GHOST
CAME TO THEM
AND THEY WERE ALL FILLED
WITH HIS POWER.

We call this Sunday Pentecost.

Book Four of "The Spiritual Way" will tell you more about the coming of The Holy Ghost at the very beginning of Jesus' Church.

For Jesus had sent The Holy Ghost to be with His Church at its very beginning AND TO REMAIN WITH IT UNTIL THE END OF THE WORLD.

So it is THE POWER OF THE HOLY GHOST which guards JESUS' CHURCH.

And we know that

THE POWER OF THE HOLY GHOST

IS THE GREATEST

AND

MOST LASTING POWER

IN THE WORLD.

✟ ✟ ✟ ✟

PAGE 16

Questions to Answer

PAGE 17

How long did Jesus stay upon earth after He rose from the dead?

Who were the first Bishops of Jesus' Church?

Whom did Jesus promise to send to His people when He went back to His Father in heaven?

How many days did Jesus' Mother, His Apostles and friends have to wait before Jesus sent The Holy Ghost?

When The Holy Ghost came to Jesus' Mother, His Apostles and His friends, what did He give them?

On what Sunday did The Holy Ghost come to Jesus' Mother, His Apostles and friends?

Whose Power guards Jesus' Church?

What have you learned in this lesson about the Power of The Holy Ghost?

How long will the Power of The Holy Ghost guard Jesus' Church?

Project Work

1. Paste a picture showing Jesus dying upon The Cross. Under the picture write one or more sentences telling what Jesus offered to His Father during His Life and most of all when He was dying upon The Cross.

2. Paste a picture of a church where you know that you may go to receive God's Grace and learn the same truths that Jesus taught. Under the picture write some sentences telling about Jesus' Church.

The Church and the Sacraments

Find the right answer to each question.

ANSWERS

His Church.
Very great love and obedience.
Through seven Sacraments.
Until the end of the world.
The Father and The Holy Ghost.
The Light of Grace; God's Grace.

QUESTIONS

1. When we want to speak about God's Love and Truth in us, what other names may we use?

2. How does Jesus' Church give God's Grace to the people?

3. How long will Jesus' Church stay upon this earth so that all people may have God's Love and Truth in them?

4. What True Teacher did Jesus leave upon the earth to keep on teaching God's Truth?

5. When Jesus was living upon this earth, He taught the people about the two other Persons of the Holy Trinity. What are the Names of these two Persons?

6. When Jesus was living upon this earth, what was He always offering to His Father?

PAGE 18

THE APOSTLES' CREED

IN THE very beginning of His Church, Jesus chose twelve men to be His great teachers. These great men were THE APOSTLES. There is a prayer called "**The Apostles' Creed.**" The Apostles' Creed IS A GREAT ACT OF FAITH.

Let us say this prayer every day.

I BELIEVE in God the Father Almighty, Creator of heaven and earth;
And in Jesus Christ, His only Son, our Lord;
Who was conceived by the Holy Ghost, born of the Virgin Mary;
Suffered under Pontius Pilate, was crucified, died and was buried;
He descended into hell; the third day He rose again from the dead;
He ascended into heaven; sitteth at the right hand of God the Father Almighty; from thence He shall come to judge the living and the dead.
I believe in the Holy Ghost; the Holy Catholic Church; the Communion of Saints;
The forgiveness of sins; the resurrection of the body; and life everlasting. Amen.

PAGE 20

JESUS' CHURCH

Music by
CORNELIA S. CRANE

Je-sus left a safe, sure way To bring to all His teach-ing clear; And if we love Him as we say, We'll love the Church He left us here.

PAGE 21

THE COMMANDMENTS OF JESUS' CHURCH

YOU have learned that Jesus left His Church upon this earth so that all people until the end of the world may have A TRUE TEACHER of God's Truth and A SURE WAY to receive God's Grace.

And Jesus' Church, our True Teacher, tells us that if we want to keep on being God's dear children, we must never fail to be at Holy Mass on Sundays and Holy Days unless there is a good reason why we cannot do this.

In the next lesson you will learn what Holy Mass means. Then you will want to take part in Holy Mass very often. And you will understand why Jesus' Church

tells us that we must **always** be present at Holy Mass on Sundays and Holy Days.

There are six Holy Days.

On the Sunday before each Holy Day, the priest will speak about it. Listen carefully so that you will be sure of the right time to go to Holy Mass on that day.

TWO COMMANDMENTS
OF JESUS' CHURCH

TO HEAR MASS ON SUNDAYS AND HOLY DAYS is the **First** Commandment of Jesus' Church.

Jesus' Church also tells us that we must show, by **NOT EATING MEAT ON FRIDAYS, THAT WE DO NOT FORGET HOW JESUS SUFFERED AND**

Jesus' Church Gives Us Six Commandments

DIED FOR US ON ONE FRIDAY LONG AGO.

This is another Commandment of Jesus' Church. And it is one way a Catholic shows his love for Jesus.

OTHER COMMANDMENTS OF JESUS' CHURCH

Jesus' Church gives us several other Commandments. And you will learn these Commandments when you study more about Jesus and His Church.

✦ ✦ ✦

Project Work

In your First Communion Notebook write "The Apostles' Creed."

Write the two Commandments of Jesus' Church that you have just learned.

Child's Name:

....

— knows the answers to the questions on pages 4, 5, 7, 9, 10, 12, 13, 17.

— has done correctly the test on page 18.

— can say or sing the verse, "Jesus' Church."

— knows who the first Bishops of Jesus' Church were.

— knows how many Sacraments there are.

— knows "The Apostles' Creed" correctly.

— knows two reasons why Jesus will leave His Church with us until the end of the world.

— knows what is meant by "God's Grace."

— knows what we receive through the Sacraments of Jesus' Church.

— knows two of the Commandments of Jesus' Church.

— knows how many Holy Days there are.

— has told in a child's own words what the book teaches about Jesus' Church and about Pentecost.

— is keeping a neat First Communion Notebook or some neat project pages approved by the teacher.

PAGE 24

....

Parent's Signature

PAGE 25

JESUS WILL STAY WITH US ALWAYS

DAVID was seven years old. He lived with his father and mother. He was their only child. David's father and mother loved God, first of all, and with their whole strength. They knew that God had given David to their care. And they loved him more than anything else God had given them.

But one day David's father became sick. David and his mother did everything to show their love and help him to get better. But David's father knew that he would soon die.

Would you like to hear what David's father said to him when he was dying?

Jesus' Priests Have Power to Offer Holy Mass

He called David to him and said: "I would like to stay with you always. But I have not the power to stay with you always.

"Only One had the power to do this.

"THIS ONE WAS JESUS.

"Jesus loved us so much that He wanted to stay with us always.

"And Jesus does stay with us always.

"For on the night before Jesus died on The Cross, He gave to His priests the power to offer Holy Mass.

"And when Jesus' priests offer the Holy Mass,

"JESUS BECOMES

"REALLY AND TRULY PRESENT.

PAGE 26

PAGE 27

"We do not see Him as He looked when He lived upon this earth, going from place to place teaching the people. But we know that He becomes present when His priests offer Holy Mass because He said that He would do this. And Jesus is God.

"I want you always to love the Holy Mass, David. For nothing else in the world is so important and wonderful.

"And always show your love for Holy Mass by taking part in it as often as you can do so. But, unless you are ill, **be sure to be present at Holy Mass on Sundays and Holy Days.**

"For if you are faithful to Holy Mass, David, I know that God will bless you."

JESUS' PRIEST USES THE POWER JESUS GAVE

IN THE middle of Holy Mass Jesus' priest uses the power which he received from Jesus when he became a priest.

And when the priest uses this power, **bread and wine are changed** into THE BODY AND BLOOD OF JESUS.

When the sacred change of the bread and wine into THE BODY AND BLOOD OF JESUS takes place, it is the time in Holy Mass which we call

THE CONSECRATION.

We cannot see any change in the bread and wine after The Consecration. For what we see still looks like bread and wine.

PAGE 28

But what
WAS
before The Consecration
bread and wine
IS
after The Consecration
THE BODY AND BLOOD OF JESUS.

And Jesus, The God-Man, becomes present then!

This sacred change of the bread and wine into the Body and Blood of Jesus, took place
THROUGH JESUS' POWER
AND JESUS' SACRED WORDS
which the priest spoke.
For Jesus' priest speaks for Jesus.

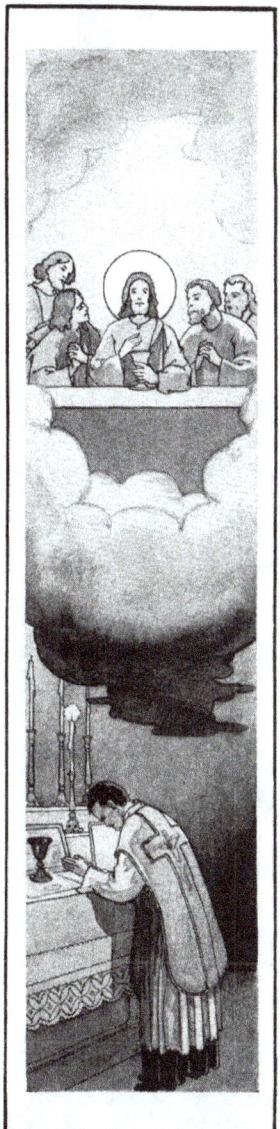

PAGE 29

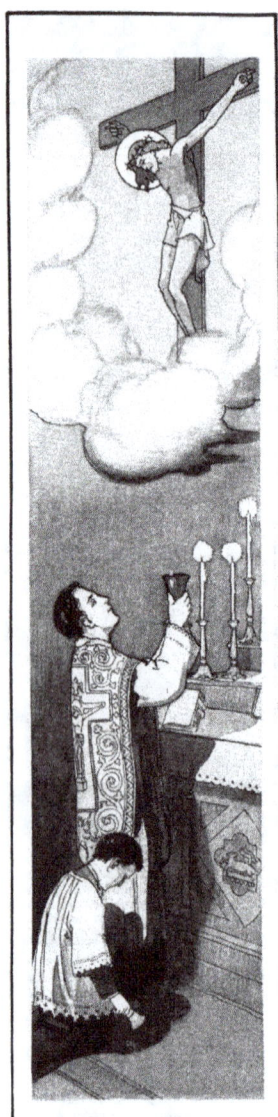

PAGE 30

ON THE CROSS
Jesus was our great High Priest.

He was offering to His Father **for us,** His Life, His Sufferings and His cruel Death with all of His great love and obedience.

AND AT THE CONSECRATION IN HOLY MASS
Jesus is also present as our great High Priest.

He offers Himself to His Father **for us,** as He did **when He was dying upon The Cross,**

His "Body which is being given" for us and His "Blood . . . . which is being shed" for us with all of HIS GREAT, GREAT LOVE AND OBEDIENCE.

But at The Consecration the priest, whom we see, speaks and acts for Jesus, Whom we cannot see.

✱ ✱ ✱

In Holy Mass, when Jesus' priest uses the power which Jesus gave him, what sacred change takes place?

Who is present when the bread and wine are changed into the Body and Blood of Jesus?

At The Consecration, for Whom does the priest speak?

On The Cross, Jesus was our great High Priest. What did He offer to His Father for us?

In what part of Holy Mass is Jesus our great High Priest?

In the middle of Holy Mass, what does Jesus offer to His Father for us?

PAGE 31

Jesus Is Our Great High Priest

AT HOLY MASS WITH JESUS

PAGE 32

YOU know that if you had been living at the time Jesus was dying upon The Cross, through love for us, you would surely have tried to go to that sacred place. And you would have stood near The Cross offering Jesus your own love and your promises to be true to Him all the days of your life.

Now you understand **that at Holy Mass,** although Jesus is not suffering as He did upon The Cross,

HE IS PRESENT!
HE IS AGAIN OFFERING HIMSELF
TO HIS FATHER
FOR US.

His "**Body** which is being given,"

PAGE 33

Jesus Offers Himself for Me

His "**Blood** . . . . which is being shed,"
and all of
His great **love** and **obedience**.

So I am sure that from now on, you will very often try to be at Holy Mass

WITH JESUS

to offer Him at this sacred time your love and your promises to be true to Him all the days of your life.

✼ ✼ ✼

If you had been living at the time that Jesus was dying upon The Cross for you, what would you have tried to do to show your love for Jesus?

Now that you understand what takes place at Holy Mass, what will you try to do to show your love for Jesus?

In Holy Mass, when Jesus is offering Himself to His Father for us, what promises will you offer Jesus?

SOME IMPORTANT ADVICE

I

At the consecration in holy mass, when Jesus comes to offer Himself to His Father for us, you will bring greater blessings upon yourself and others **if you also**

OFFER JESUS TO HIS FATHER,

His "Body which is being given,"

His "Blood .... which is being shed,"

with His great, great love and His obedience, "even to the death of The Cross."

II

And you will show that you love God **above all,** if at The Consecration

YOU ASK JESUS

TO OFFER WITH HIS LIFE,
your life,
WITH HIS LOVE AND OBEDIENCE,
your love and obedience.

✦ ✦ ✦

At Holy Mass, how can you bring greater blessings upon yourself and others?

At Holy Mass, how can you show that you love God above all?

✦ ✦ ✦ ✦

JESUS, you know, is God's Own "Beloved Son."

And Jesus' Father is always "well pleased" with Him.

Jesus is the highest, the greatest and the holiest One Who ever lived upon this

PAGE 35

WHY WE OFFER PRAYERS THROUGH JESUS

PAGE 36

earth. And when you are older and are reading other books about Jesus, they will help you to understand better than you do now why we say that Jesus is

THE HEAD OF US ALL.

Through Jesus we are made holy with God's Love and Truth. And when Jesus, THE GREAT AND HOLY HEAD OF US ALL, **is present during Holy Mass,** offering Himself to His Father for us, His Father turns toward us with love.

He looks upon us as very dear children.

And because Jesus is THE HEAD OF US ALL, He is pleased to hear our prayers.

He is pleased to bless us and to help us.

HOLY COM- MUNION

AFTER the bread and wine have been changed into The Body and Blood of Jesus, and Jesus has offered to His Father for us His Body and His Blood, with all of His great love and obedience, then He wants to come to us **to make us holy** with His Love and Truth. What was, before The Consecration, round white bread, is, after The Consecration, A HOLY HOST.

And when we receive The Holy Host,
JESUS
COMES TO LIVE WITHIN US.
Receiving Jesus in The Holy Host
is called
RECEIVING HOLY COMMUNION.

THE FIRST PART OF HOLY MASS

AT THE beginning of Holy Mass, keep thanking God for having sent Jesus to this earth to offer for us such great love and obedience that He more than made up for the turning away from God of our first parents and all other people.

Tell Him that you are sorry for every time that you did not give Him love and obedience, and that you will try very hard to obey Jesus' two great Commandments of Love.

Then ask Him to bless you, and to let you have more of The Light of Grace in you. For this is the best way to prepare for the great moment when Jesus will be

Preparing for the Coming of Jesus

present in The Holy Host, offering for us His Body and His Blood with His great love and obedience, as He did when He was dying upon The Cross.

And if you try to prepare well for this great moment, you will be very pleasing to Jesus when He comes to you in The Holy Host.

✢ ✢ ✢

    Why is Jesus' Father always "well pleased" with all that Jesus offers?

    Why is Jesus' Father pleased with our gifts when Jesus offers them?

    After The Consecration, what is the round white bread called?

    When we receive The Holy Host, Who comes to live within us?

    When we say that we receive Holy Communion, what do we mean?

THE LAST PART OF HOLY MASS

AFTER you have received Jesus in The Holy Host, **thank Him** for coming to you.

Ask Him to give you more and more of His Love and Truth so that you will keep on growing more like Him in holiness.

Ask Him for many other good things for yourself, for your father and mother and for all those whom you love.

And say many sincere Acts of Faith, Hope and Love.

✶ ✶ ✶

Tell some other child what to do during The First Part of Holy Mass; during The Last Part of Holy Mass.

PAGE 40

AN ACT OF FAITH

* * *

My Jesus, I believe that when I receive the Holy Host, you come to live within me.

AN ACT OF HOPE

* * *

My Jesus, I hope to see you face to face when I die.

AN ACT OF LOVE

* * *

My Jesus, I love you. Teach me to act more like you as I grow day by day.

Acts of Faith, Hope and Love

PAGE 42

A Test

In your First Communion Notebook draw a three-story house.

Draw three windows in each story.

There are three stories in your house and there are three parts to the Holy Mass.

Questions about the Beginning of Holy Mass

Write the answers to these questions in the windows of the ground floor of your house.

At the beginning of Holy Mass, about Whom should you be thinking?

At the beginning of Holy Mass, you should tell God that you are sorry. Why should you be sorry?

You are preparing for the sacred moment when Jesus will be offering Himself to His Father for us, as He did on The Cross.

Why is it important to make good use of the time given to The First Part of Holy Mass?

Questions about the Middle of Holy Mass

Write the answers to these questions in the windows of the middle floor of your house.

Who gave Jesus' priests the power to change bread and wine into His Body and Blood?

In the middle of Holy Mass what does Jesus offer to His Father for us?

Receiving Jesus in The Holy Host has a special name. What is the name?

Questions about the Last Part of Holy Mass

Write the answers to these questions in the windows of the top floor of your house.

After Jesus comes to you in The Holy Host, what should you say to Him for all the good things He has given to you?

What should you ask for those you love?

What Acts should you say?

Project Work

Write the Acts of Faith, Hope and Love in your First Communion Notebook or on a project page.

Learn these acts.

Paste a picture showing Jesus with His Apostles on the night before He died. Under the picture write a sentence telling what power Jesus gave to His priests on that night.

PAGE 43

PAGE 44

Child's Name:

....

— knows what Jesus did for us on the night before He died which showed that He loved us and had great power.

— knows Who becomes really and truly present when Jesus' priests offer the Holy Mass.

— knows at what time in Holy Mass Jesus becomes really and truly present.

— knows what Jesus does for us during Holy Mass.

— knows why David's father wanted him to be faithful in his love for Holy Mass.

— can say correctly the Acts of Faith, Hope and Love given on page 41.

— can answer correctly the questions in the tests on pages 31, 33, 35 and 39.

— can tell in a child's own words what this book teaches about the Holy Mass.

— can say Jesus' two Great Commandments of Love.

— has kept a neat First Communion Notebook or has finished some neat project pages approved by the teacher.

....

Parent's Signature

BOOK FIVE

TOM AND ANN ASK QUESTIONS

Tom and Ann were preparing for
THEIR FIRST CONFESSION.
They asked many questions.
Perhaps you would like to ask the same questions
that Tom and Ann asked.

If you read *Book Five*

YOU WILL FIND OUT WHAT QUESTIONS
THEY ASKED.

YOU WILL ALSO FIND OUT
HOW THEIR MOTHER ANSWERED
TOM'S AND ANN'S QUESTIONS.

Approved by the National Center of the Confraternity
of Christian Doctrine

GOD'S LOVE AND TRUTH IN US

OM and Ann were talking one day with their mother about their First Holy Communion.

Tom said: "I want to be like Jesus. What shall I do to be more like Jesus?"

"JESUS IS ALL-HOLY," answered their mother. "And to be more like Jesus, you must have more of God's Love and Truth in you."

Then Ann asked: "What can I do to have more of God's Love and Truth in me?"

Their mother answered: "You know that God, Our Father, is All-Love and All-Truth. And you have learned that Jesus,

God's Own Son, gives us of God's Love and Truth THROUGH THE SACRAMENTS OF THE CHURCH HE LEFT US."

❧ ❧ ❧ ❧

THE SACRAMENT OF BAPTISM

IN 'THE Story of Our First Parents' you read that God's Grace was not in you at the beginning of your life.

"You were then in the state of original sin.

"But when you received the Sacrament of Baptism, God let you share in His Love and Truth for the first time. THIS MADE YOU GOD'S CHILD.

PAGE 2

"At that moment The Holy Ghost came to live within you.

"And at that moment you became A 'TEMPLE OF THE LIVING GOD.'

"No one can receive the Sacrament of Baptism more than once. And everyone must be baptized before he can receive the other Sacraments."

✦ ✦ ✦ ✦

"AT BAPTISM everyone must have a godfather or a godmother. We call the godfather or godmother a SPONSOR.

"And when the one being baptized is a

THE SPONSOR AT BAPTISM

baby, the sponsor answers the questions which the priest asks the baby.

"When you study more about the Sacrament of Baptism, you will learn what questions the sponsor must answer and everything else the sponsor must do for the baby."

✶ ✶ ✶

At the beginning of your life you were in the state of original sin. Tell what this statement means. When you were baptized what did you share for the first time?

When did you become God's child?

When you were baptized, Who came to live within you?

At the moment of your Baptism, Whose temple were you?

Which Sacrament must everyone receive first?

PAGE 5

THE SACRAMENT OF CONFIRMATION

"As I HAVE just told you, when we were baptized we became 'temples of the Living God.'

"And the Holy Ghost gave us of His Power at Baptism so that we could know God, Our Father, and love Him as He wants all of His children to know and to love Him.

"So you see that the Power which The Holy Ghost gave us at Baptism helps us to keep on being holy 'temples of the Living God.'

"But there is another Sacrament which is sometimes called the Sacra-

The Holy Ghost Gives New Power

ment of **The Holy Ghost.** For when we receive this Sacrament, The Holy Ghost gives us MORE of the same Power which He gave us at Baptism.

"And He also gives us New Power!

"At another time when we are talking together, I will tell you what this NEW POWER will do for you when you receive The Sacrament of The Holy Ghost.

"You have heard other children talking about CONFIRMATION.

"And it is THE SACRAMENT OF CONFIRMATION which will give you this NEW POWER.

"For it is THE SACRAMENT OF CONFIRMATION which is sometimes

called THE SACRAMENT OF THE HOLY GHOST."

✦ ✦ ✦ ✦

"YOU remember that I told you that you could not receive any other Sacrament unless you had been baptized. So you could not receive the Sacrament of Confirmation unless you had been baptized. For the Light of God's Grace must be in you when you receive the Sacrament of Confirmation.

"But you have both been baptized.

"And you will both receive the Sacrament of Confirmation soon after you know

PAGE 7

A SOLDIER OF JESUS' CHURCH

more about the other Sacraments of Jesus' Church.

"In our last talk together, you learned that when you receive the Sacrament of Confirmation The Holy Ghost will give you **new Power.**

"I promised you then that I would tell you what this new Power will do for you.

"And I will tell you now.

"**The new Power which you will receive at Confirmation will make you very brave and strong to do what God wants you to do.**

"Brave and strong to suffer for God.

"And brave and strong to work for God.

PAGE 9

"For this Sacrament will make you a soldier of Jesus' Church.

"The Sacrament of Confirmation can be received but once.

"You will remember that this was also true of the Sacrament of Baptism."

↗ ↗ ↗ ↗

"**W**HEN the Bishop gives anyone the Sacrament of Confirmation, we say that he CONFIRMS that person.

"To **Confirm** means to **make strong.**

"When the Bishop confirms anyone, he extends his hands over the one being confirmed and says some prayers asking

WHEN THE BISHOP CONFIRMS

PAGE 10

The Holy Ghost to give to this one more of Himself, more of The Light of Grace and more of His great Gifts.

"Then, with holy oil called chrism, he makes The Sign of The Cross on the forehead of the one being confirmed, saying: **'I confirm thee . . . . In the name of The Father, and of The Son, and of The Holy Ghost.'**

"After this the Bishop strikes the person gently on the cheek as a sign that he must be strong and brave enough to stand suffering for God.

"Then he says: **'Peace be with thee.'**

"After the Bishop says the prayer 'Peace be with thee,' he says other prayers

"Peace Be with Thee"

asking God to bless the one being confirmed all the days of his life, and to take him to heaven when he dies."

Tom said: "I hope we can receive the Sacrament of Confirmation soon."

Their mother answered: "When you and Ann know well all the lessons in **'A Little Child's First Communion,'** I shall then review these Confirmation lessons which we are now having and give you some more lessons from another book written for older children. It is **Book Four** of **'The Spiritual Way.'**

"The lessons from that book will teach you more about the Sacrament of Confirmation.

"You will then learn about seven Great Gifts.

"And these Great Gifts are seven different kinds of Power which The Holy Ghost gives to us.

"THEY ARE CALLED
THE GIFTS OF THE HOLY GHOST."

↟ ↟ ↟ ↟

YOUR CONFIRMATION SPONSOR

"YOU must have a sponsor when you are confirmed as you did when you were baptized.

"The priest or your parents will help you to choose a good sponsor. And a good

PAGE 12

Your Sponsor Will Help You

sponsor is one who is able to advise you in the right way if, as you grow older, you need someone to help you to be true to Jesus and a brave soldier of His Kingdom."

Tell other children what you have read in this book about the Sacraments of Baptism and Confirmation.

A Test

Parts of sentences are given in each list.
Put the right parts of the sentences together and ask someone at home to see if your sentences are right.

LIST ONE

Confirmation is sometimes called ....
When you receive the Sacrament of Confirmation, The Holy Ghost will give ....

The Power of The Holy Ghost helps us to be ....

To confirm means ....

Confirmation is usually given by ....

The Sacrament of Confirmation ....

The Bishop extends his hands over the one being confirmed, asking ....

The Bishop strikes the person gently on the cheek as a sign that he must ....

The Bishop makes The Sign of the Cross on the forehead with chrism, saying: ....

At last the Bishop asks God ....

LIST TWO

................will make you a soldier of Jesus' Church.

................strong and brave and true for God.

................The Holy Ghost to give him all His Gifts.

................stand suffering for God.

................to make strong.

................"I confirm thee . . . . In the name of The Father, and of The Son, and of The Holy Ghost.

................to bless the one being confirmed all the days of his life.

................you more of Himself, more of The Light of Grace, and more of His Seven Great Gifts.

................a Bishop.

................the Sacrament of The Holy Ghost.

PAGE 14

SIN AND CONFESSION

SEVERAL days after their mother had been talking with Tom and Ann about the two wonderful Sacraments called Baptism and Confirmation, Ann said:

"Mother, we had a happy time the day you told us about Baptism and Confirmation. So please tell us about another Sacrament."

Their mother said that she would be glad to tell them about another Sacrament of Jesus' Church. And this is what their mother said to Tom and Ann that day:

"Tom, you know that when you were baptized you became 'a temple of the Living God.'

God Is All Love

"And you know, Ann, that when you were baptized you also became 'a temple of the Living God.'

"But for several years after Baptism, you were both too little to know 'the Living God.'

"You were too little to know what was FOR GOD and what was AGAINST GOD.

"But now that you are both old enough to know that God is All-Love and All-Truth, you are old enough to know

"WHAT IS FOR GOD

"AND

"WHAT IS AGAINST GOD.

> All Sins Are Bad

"And any act against God is called a sin.

"All sins are bad.

"All sins take away some likeness to Jesus, our Model, Who is All-Holy.

"And all sins mean that the one who commits the sin IS NOT GIVING

"TO 'THE LIVING GOD'

"ALL THE LOVE

"WHICH SHOULD BE GIVEN

"TO HIM."

✦ ✦ ✦ ✦

LITTLE SINS

"LITTLE sins '**grieve**' This Holy One.

"SO IT IS VERY SAD when one who is 'a temple of the Living God' commits little sins.

"But 'the Living God' LOVES each one who is His temple.

"And This Holy One will keep on dwelling within His temple unless the sin committed is very bad!"

✓ ✓ ✓ ✓

PAGE 18

VERY BAD SINS

"IF YOU should ever commit a very bad sin, that would be the saddest thing that could ever happen to you.

"For a very bad sin would take away all of your holiness. Then there would be none of God's Grace in you.

"You would no longer be a 'temple of the Living God.' And if you should die at a time when there was none of God's Grace in you, you could not be in heaven, Jesus' kingdom.

"For all people who have turned away from God, and have none of God's Grace in them when they die, must be where all the bad people are."

GOOD ANGELS

"YOU have learned that there are ANGELS. For you have read about the bright and beautiful angel who let Mary know that God wanted her to be the Mother of His Own Son, and about the angel who let Saint Joseph know that God wanted him to take care of Jesus and Mary.

"These are GOOD ANGELS. And there are many good angels.

"The good angels love God.

"They want to serve Him

"AND THEY WANT TO HELP US."

🗲 🗲 🗲 🗲

PAGE 20

BAD ANGELS

"But there are also BAD ANGELS. Long ago these bad angels turned away from God. They did not love Him. And they would not serve Him.

"So they could not be in heaven.

"They are called devils.

"The devils are in hell.

"And everyone who has turned away from God, and at the time he dies has none of God's Grace in him, will be in hell with the devils forever.

"The devils or bad angels try to make us turn away from God, just as they did. And they do not want us to keep The Light of Grace shining in us.

The Devils Turned Away from God

"When the devil is trying to make us do what would not be pleasing to God, Our Father, we say that he is tempting us.

"Now you know why it is very necessary for us ALWAYS to GUARD WELL GOD'S GIFT OF GRACE.

’ ’ ’

What is meant by a sin?

When anyone sins, what does he refuse to give to "the Living God"?

Why is it very sad when a child of God is not sorry when he commits little sins?

If anyone should commit a very bad sin, what holy gift is not his any longer?

What people cannot be in Jesus' kingdom when they die?

When a person who has turned away from God dies, with whom must he be forever?

What do the devils want us to do?

What do the good angels want us to do?

PAGE 22

THE POWER TO FORGIVE SINS

"YOU know that Jesus loves us.

"He wants us holy, with God's Grace in us. And He also wants us to grow in holiness.

"**So He gave to all of His priests the power to forgive our sins if we are truly sorry for them.**

"And when our sins have been forgiven, by one of Jesus' priests, we are sure that we are holy or growing in holiness.

"For if we had none of God's Grace in us before our sins were forgiven, Jesus then gives us this holy gift. But if we already have God's Grace in us, Jesus gives us MORE of this holy gift."

THE SACRAMENT OF PENANCE

"WHEN Jesus' priest uses the power which Jesus gave to him and forgives our sins, we have received another Sacrament of Jesus' Church."

Ann asked: "What is the name of this Sacrament?"

"It is called the SACRAMENT OF PENANCE," their mother answered. **"And you will receive the Sacrament of Penance when you make a good Confession."**

"Just what do we do at Confession?" asked Tom.

Their mother answered: "Confession is the telling of our sins to one of Jesus'

PAGE 24

PAGE 25

The Meaning of Confession

priests so that, with the power Jesus gave him, he will forgive these sins.

"And when you make a good Confession, you have done one of the things that Jesus' Church tells you to do before receiving Jesus in your First Holy Communion."

✝ ✝ ✝

Because Jesus wants our sins forgiven so that we may always be holy, what power did He give to His priests?

Could Jesus' priests forgive our sins if we were not truly sorry for them?

When our sins have been forgiven by one of Jesus' priests, what holy gift does Jesus give us?

When our sins have been forgiven by one of Jesus' priests, what Sacrament have we received?

Tell what you have learned about Confession.

The Sacrament of the Holy Eucharist

"WHEN Jesus comes to you in Holy Communion, you will receive another Sacrament called The Holy Eucharist.

"And each time that you receive Jesus lovingly in the Sacrament of The Holy Eucharist, there will be more of God's Love and Truth in you."

*　*　*

When Jesus comes to you in Holy Communion what Sacrament do you receive?

At Baptism, God's Love and Truth were in you for the first time. After your First Communion what Sacrament may you receive often, so that there will be more and more of God's Love and Truth in you?

GOD WANTS ME HOLY

Music by
CORNELIA S. CRANE

God made the pret-ty flow'rs and trees;
God made the world all love-li-ness;
God loves me more than all of these; He
gives me of His ho-li-ness.

.... has studied **Book Five** and has done correctly all the work that is asked for on this page.

Write in your First Communion Notebook or on project pages:

— The name of the first Sacrament you received.

— The name of the Sacrament you receive when you make a good Confession.

— The name of the Sacrament you receive when Jesus comes to you in Holy Communion.

— The name of the Sacrament which will make you very brave and strong to do what you know God wants you to do, even if this means great suffering for you.

— One or more sentences telling why you are happy to know that you were baptized.

— Some other sentences telling why you will be happy to receive each of the other Sacraments.

— The test on pages 13 and 14.

— Three reasons why all sins are bad.

— Some sentences about the good angels and the bad angels.

PAGE 28

....
Parent's Signature

PAGE 29

Questions about Confession

ONE day after dinner, when Tom and Ann and their mother were talking together, their mother asked:

"When did the priest say that you would make your first Confession?"

"Next week," answered Tom, "and I do not know yet how to tell my sins."

"Perhaps I can help you," their mother said.

"Let us talk for a while about Confession.

"First of all, before you go to Confession, try to take a little while alone with God.

"God loves you very much more than

PAGE 30

He loves the whole world with all the flowers and trees and plants which grow upon the earth, and the animals which live upon it.

"God wants you to keep The Light of Grace in you.

"And God wants you to grow more like Jesus.

"Jesus is All-Holy. And you want to grow in holiness.

"SO BE STILL FOR A LITTLE WHILE.

"Then ask The Holy Ghost to help you to know everything you have done against God's Love and Truth.

PAGE 31

An Act of Contrition

"For remember, God Our Father is All-Love and All-Truth, and anything you do against Him is a sin.

"Ask God to make you truly sorry for all your sins.

"And when you tell God that you are sorry for your sins, you make an Act of Contrition."

✝ ✝ ✝ ✝

TOM'S AND ANN'S ACT OF CONTRITION

O my God, All-Love and All-Truth,
   I am sorry for all my sins
      For I love You!
         I firmly resolve, with the help of Your Grace,
            Not to sin again.

Now let us think for a while

ABOUT THESE QUESTIONS:

1. Have I always spoken about God with love and respect?
   Have I always used the name of Jesus with love?

2. Have I always shown that I am a true child of our Heavenly Father by talking respectfully and lovingly to Him in my prayers morning and evening?

3. Have I always obeyed Jesus' Church by taking part in Holy Mass every Sunday and Holy Day when I was able to do this? And have I always tried very hard to be in the church at the beginning of Holy Mass?

4. During Holy Mass did I think about the coming of Jesus in The Holy Host with Faith, Hope and Love? In the middle of Holy Mass, did I remember that Jesus is present offering Himself for us, His Body and His Blood, with His great, great love and obedience, as He did upon The Cross?

5. Have I ever refused to obey the Commandment of Jesus' Church which tells me not to eat meat on Friday in memory of Jesus' death?

6. Have I disobeyed my father or mother or anyone else whom I knew I should obey?

7. Have I ever told a lie by saying something about a person or thing which I knew was not the truth?

PAGE 32

8. Have I ever thought that I was better than another child because I had prettier clothes? Or have I thought that I was better than another child because I found it easier to learn my lessons? If I thought these things made me better, I was proud.

9. When things did not go as I liked, was I cross? Did I show a disagreeable temper? Did I say or do anything unkind or disagreeable?

10. Have I ever taken or kept anything which I did not have a right to take or keep?

11. Have I wanted very much, and kept on wanting very much, things that I had no right to have? Have I been sad because another person had something that I wanted for myself?
    Have I been unfair to another person who had something that I wanted for myself?

12. When I was baptized, The Holy Ghost came to dwell within me.
    Then my body became a "temple of the Living God." Have I ever had anything to do with any man or woman, boy or girl, who did not respect "the Living God" and the home where He is dwelling?

13. Have I myself ever been disrespectful to The Holy Ghost and to His sacred home by using my eyes to look at evil pictures? By using my ears to listen to evil words? By using my hands to write evil words, to draw evil pictures, or to do other evil things? By using my tongue to speak evil words?

PAGE 33

A GAME OF CASES

ONE evening when Tom and Ann were talking with their father and mother, they asked to play a game.

Their mother said: "Would you like to play a game of cases?"

Tom and Ann said that they would like to learn that game.

Their mother said: "This is the way to play the game.

"Mother will give the case.

"Tom and Ann will read the questions on pages 32 and 33.

"Then they will judge the number of the question which goes with each case. Each one will write the number on a separate piece of paper. Then father will be the final judge and keep Tom's and Ann's score."

PAGE 35

⚹ ⚹ ⚹

[1] Peter's mother made an apple pie for dinner at noon. Peter's big brother James never came home for dinner. His mother saved him a nice piece of pie. When Peter came home from school, he ate the pie. He did not know that it was being saved for James.

But when his mother asked him about the pie, Peter said that he did not know anything about it. This was a sin.

What is the number of the question that asks about this sin?

⚹ ⚹ ⚹

[2] Paul and Anthony, with several other boys were playing ball. While Anthony was running he dropped his knife near Paul. Paul picked up the knife to give it to Anthony. But he liked the knife so much that he kept it. This was a sin.

What is the number of the question that asks about this sin?

The Temple of the Living God

3 Arthur knew that his body was a "temple of the Living God."

He played every afternoon with two other boys who lived near him.

After a while these boys looked at evil pictures and said things and wrote things and did things which Arthur knew showed disrespect to The Holy Ghost and to the home where He was dwelling.

Arthur did not play with these boys any more.

What is the number of the question which asks about being with anyone who does not show respect to The Holy Ghost and to His sacred home?

What is the number of the question which asks you if you have ever been disrespectful to The Holy Ghost and to the sacred temple where He dwells by the way you used your eyes? your ears? your hands? your tongue?

✶ ✶ ✶

4 Margaret knew that she should be present at Holy Mass on August 15. Margaret's father was dead and her mother had to go to work. Her mother went to Holy Mass early.

PAGE 36

PAGE 37

But she came home and before going to work called Margaret. Margaret said that she would get up and go to Holy Mass. But Margaret did not go to Holy Mass. This was a sin.

What is the number of the question that asks about this sin?

⚡ ⚡ ⚡

5 The other day I heard Frank speak the Holy Name of Jesus when he was fighting. This was a sin for Frank.

What is the number of the question that asks about this sin?

⚡ ⚡ ⚡

6. Edward was invited to George's birthday party on Friday afternoon. George was not a Catholic, and ham and chicken sandwiches were served at the party. Edward knew the Commandment of Jesus' Church about not eating meat on Fridays in memory of Jesus' cruel death. He remembered that it was Friday. But he was afraid that the other children would ask him why he did not eat the sandwiches. So he ate some of them. He disobeyed a Commandment of Jesus' Church.

What is the number of the question that asks about this sin?

⚡ ⚡ ⚡

What We Should Do at Holy Mass

7 Jane was going to Holy Mass on Sunday morning. She wanted Ruth to walk to Holy Mass with her. She stopped at Ruth's house but Ruth was not ready. She waited for her. Both Jane and Ruth were very late for Holy Mass.

While they were at Holy Mass, instead of preparing for the coming of Jesus, they talked about the dresses of the other girls.

What is the number of the question that asks about being on time for Holy Mass?

What is the number of the question that asks about what we should do during Holy Mass?

8 While Kathleen's mother was doing everything to make her happy, Kathleen was never cross or disagreeable. But one day when Kathleen's friend Dorothy wanted Kathleen to come over to her house to play, Kathleen's mother said that she wanted her to stay at home that afternoon. Then Kathleen stamped her feet and showed a very bad temper.

This was a sin.

What is the number of the question that asks about this sin?

PAGE 38

PAGE 39

Showing Love and Respect in Prayer

9 Sarah's mother knew that Julia was sick with scarlet fever. So she told Sarah that she must not go to Julia's house to play for several weeks. One day Sarah was passing Julia's house. She saw the door open and went in to play with her.

The doctor came and found them playing. The doctor told Sarah's mother. He gave her medicine to give to Sarah and told her to keep Sarah in the house for nine days.

It was a sin for Sarah to disobey her mother.

What is the number of the question that asks about this sin?

✦ ✦ ✦

10 Helen always said her morning and night prayers. But she did not think of what she was saying. She thought about school or parties or other things. This means that although Helen was talking to God, she was not giving Him love and respect.

What is the number of the question that asks about showing love and respect to God while saying our prayers?

✦ ✦ ✦

Pride and Envy Make People Very Unhappy

11 Richard had to work very hard to learn numbers and sometimes he made mistakes. John learned numbers very easily. So John thought that he was better than Richard. John was proud. It is a sin to be proud.

What is the number of the question that asks about this sin?

12 Betty did her school work neatly and well. The teacher was pleased with Betty. And all the children liked her.

Lucy did not do her work well. She was lazy and selfish and the teacher was not pleased with her.

But Lucy was sad and kept on being sad because the teacher marked Betty A. She was sad, too, because she saw that the other children all liked Betty.

So when the teacher gave out the report cards, Lucy would not speak to Betty and she said mean things about her to the other children.

It was a sin for Lucy to keep on being sad because people were pleased with Betty. It was a sin called envy.

What is the number of the question that asks about this sin?

PAGE 40

TOM AND ANN GO TO CONFESSION

"MOTHER," said Tom, "I am going to Confession this afternoon. Before I go, tell me again exactly what to do."

Ann said: "I want to know just what to do, too. So tell us both."

Contrition

Their mother answered:

"The first thing to remember is that every time you choose to sin, you show that you do not love God more than anyone or anything else. So, of course, you will be very sorry for these sins.

"And you will make a good Act of Contrition."

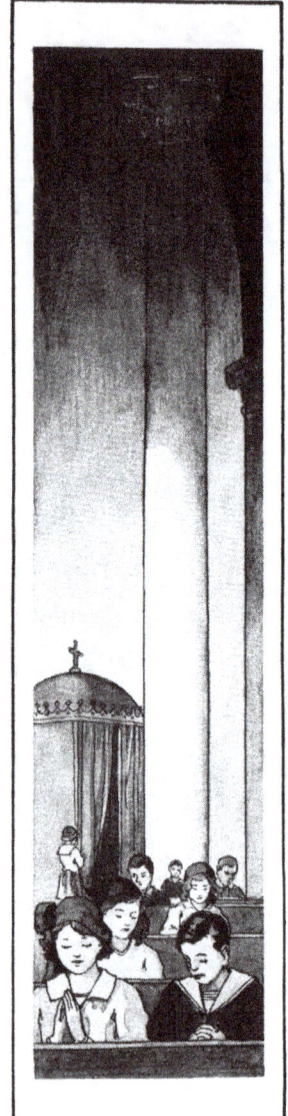

While Waiting

"After you know the sins that you should tell in Confession and have made a good Act of Contrition, wait patiently until your turn comes to go into the confessional. And while you are waiting, talk lovingly to Jesus, telling Him what you will try to do to be more like Him. But at this time do not talk to the other children."

Beginning Confession

"When your turn comes, go into the confessional and when the priest opens the little sliding door, make The Sign of the Cross and say: 'Bless me, Father.'

What We Should Do at Confession

"And the priest will give you his blessing.

"Then say: 'I confess to Almighty God and to you, Father, that I have sinned.'

"If you are going to Confession for the first time, say: 'This is my first Confession.'

"But when you go to Confession after that, do not say: 'This is my first Confession.' Say: 'My last Confession was one week ago, or two weeks ago,' or whatever number of days or weeks it was since your last Confession."

Telling Your Sins

"The next thing to do is to tell your sins. And you should tell your sins so that the priest will understand them.

"You must also tell the priest the number of times you committed any sin that you think is very bad.

"This means that you must tell whether you committed this sin once or twice, or very often, or only once in a while.

"If you should begin to be afraid to tell some sin that you think is very bad, remember that you want to come away from Confession filled with God's Love and Truth. **So you must be sure not to pay attention to your fear.**"

Ann said: "If I am not quite sure whether something that I have said or done is a sin or not, then what shall I do?"

Her mother answered: "If you have done something and do not know whether it is a sin or not, you should tell the priest when you go to Con-

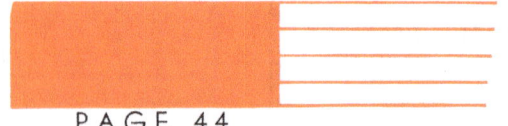

PAGE 44

fession. **For in Confession the priest takes Jesus' place.**

"And if you should find that some sin is hard to tell, I think that it is best for you to tell that sin first.

"But if you do not know how to tell some sin, I am sure that the priest will help you if you let him know that you do not know how to tell it. If you should really forget a sin while you are at Confession, tell this sin in your very next Confession, explaining that you forgot it."

After Telling Your Sins to the Priest

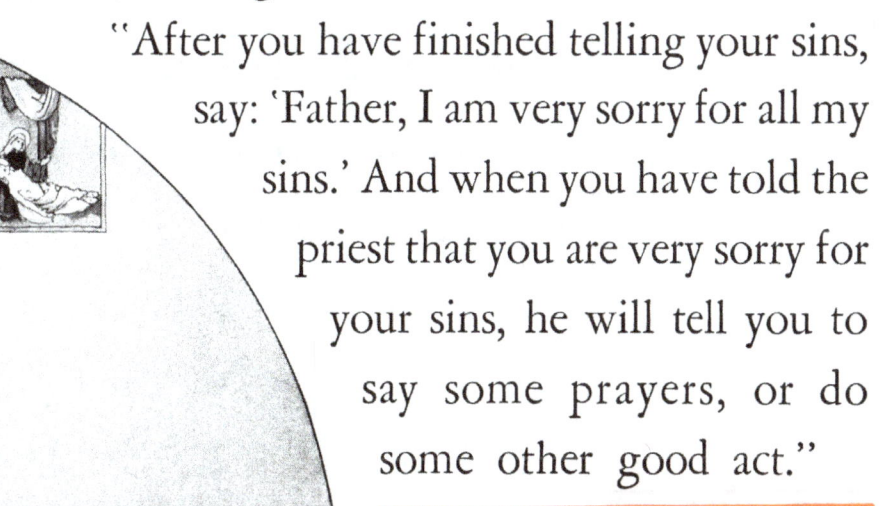

"After you have finished telling your sins, say: 'Father, I am very sorry for all my sins.' And when you have told the priest that you are very sorry for your sins, he will tell you to say some prayers, or do some other good act."

PAGE 45

The Priest Uses the Power Jesus Gave Him

Your Penance

"The prayers which the priest, in Confession, tells you to say, or any other good act which he tells you to do, is called YOUR PENANCE."

The Priest Uses His Power

"After the priest has given you a penance, he will tell you to make an Act of Contrition. **And while you are saying the Act of Contrition, he will use the power Jesus gave him to forgive your sins.** So be sure to say your Act of Contrition with very much love, and promise Jesus that you will try to be more like Him."

PAGE 46

After Confession

"When your Confession is over, it is well to go at once to another part of the church, a little away from the other children. For of course, you should perform your penance before you leave the church if you can do this.

"And I know that you will want to spend some time THANKING GOD for letting you make this Confession and for giving you more of His Grace.

"You will learn a little later why you should always perform your penance with faith and love."

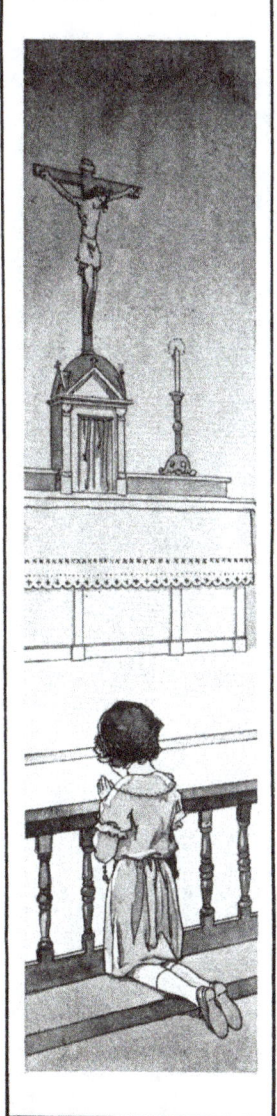

PAGE 47

The Reason for the Penance Given in Confession

"YOU know that every sin is an act against God, Who is All-Love and All-Truth.

"AND EVERY SIN ALWAYS BRINGS SUFFERING. This suffering may come at the very time the sin is committed or it may come later.

"When you are older you will learn much more about the suffering which sin causes.

"But now I am sure that you will be happy to know what Jesus' Church tells us about the penance which the priest gives in Confession.

Jesus Gave Great Power to His Church

"For Jesus' Church tells us that if we PERFORM with FAITH AND LOVE THE PENANCE which the priest gives us in Confession, this penance will take the place of some of the suffering which our sins have caused.

"And you have learned that Jesus gave great power to His Church."

Tom and Ann said: "Thank you, Mother."

.............has studied Book Five and has done correctly all the work that is asked for in this test.

A Test

Make three columns in your First Communion Notebook. Mark the columns A, B and C.

In the A column write three sentences which tell what you should do before you go into the confessional.

In the B column write five sentences which tell what you should do while you are in the confessional.

In the C column write three sentences which tell what you should do after Confession.

1. "Father, my last Confession was one week ago."
2. The priest says: "Make a good Act of Contrition."
3. Thank God for giving you more of His Grace.
4. You must tell your sins so that the priest will understand them.
5. You should wait patiently until your turn comes.
6. Tell the priest about how many times you committed each sin.
7. "Bless me, Father. I confess to Almighty God and to you, Father, that I have sinned."
8. You must know your sins.
9. Say your penance with much love.
10. Thank God for letting you make this Confession.
11. You must be truly sorry for your sins.

PAGE 50

A Project Just for Yourself

(Copy this page. Mark your score. But you need not show your marks to anyone.)

TRYING TO BE MORE LIKE JESUS EACH DAY

Count ten if you can answer **yes** to the question. At the end of each day add your tens.

	PERFECT SCORE	Sunday	Monday	Tuesday	Wednesday	Thursday	Friday	Saturday
1. Have I done one good deed that I need not have done?	10							
2. Did I think of God and say an Act of Love at least twice during the day?	10							
3. Did I obey home and school rules when no one was looking, as well as at other times?	10							
4. Did I do all my lessons and other work carefully today?	10							
5. Was I kind and polite to every one?	10							
	50							

A Test

Ask your father or mother to write your name in the blank spaces and to sign this page.

................knows correctly the Act of Contrition on page 31.

................knows what this book teaches about the penance given in Confession.

................knows how to prepare for Confession; what to do in Confession; what to do after Confession.

................knows the names of four Sacraments.

................can say or sing the verse "God Wants Me Holy."

................knows what this book teaches about the angels.

................knows what this book teaches about Confirmation.

....
Parent's Signature

BOOK SIX

A VISITOR, GREAT AND HOLY

Tom and Ann were expecting AN IMPORTANT VISIT. It was to take place on a feast day which was coming very soon.

They had spent several months getting ready. And now they wanted this visit so much that it was hard for them to wait for that great day to come.

The stories in this book tell the very last THINGS THAT TOM AND ANN DID TO PREPARE for the important visit which they were expecting.

Read these stories and tell your classmates what to do when they are expecting a visit from THIS GREAT AND HOLY ONE.

Approved by the National Center of the Confraternity of Christian Doctrine

PAGE 1

JESUS IS COMING

JESUS was The Visitor, Great and Holy, Whom Tom and Ann were expecting.

So Tom and Ann spent the evening before their First Communion Day THINKING ABOUT JESUS and His holy visit to them on the very next morning.

They remembered the Acts of Faith, Hope and Love which they had learned TO GREET JESUS on His coming.

Tom and Ann knew that Jesus was coming to make them more and more holy with His Own Love and Truth. So they thought about the THANK YOU they would say to Him.

They also thought about many, many other things they would say to Jesus WHEN HE CAME TO THEM IN THE MORNING.

Of course, they prepared so that everything about them would be clean and neat.

They talked with their father and mother. And they asked their father to tell them just what to do on the morning of their First Holy Communion.

✝ ✝ ✝

In the next story you will learn what their father told them.

✝ ✝ ✝ ✝

A Test

There are five sentences in this test.

The first part of each sentence is:

> **The evening before you receive Holy Communion, you should prepare for Jesus' holy visit by** . . . .

The middle of each sentence is in *Group One*. The end of each sentence is in *Group Two*.

Put the three parts of each sentence together.

GROUP ONE
. . . thinking . . .
. . . talking . . .
. . . remembering . . .
. . . thinking about what you will say to . . .
. . . thinking about the Acts . . .

GROUP TWO
. . . to Jesus.
. . . that Jesus is coming to make you more holy with His Love and Truth.
. . . Jesus when He comes to you in the morning.
. . . of Faith, Hope and Love which you have learned.
. . . about Jesus.

WHAT THEIR FATHER TOLD TOM AND ANN

"WHEN Tom and Ann were talking with their father, he said:

"Jesus' Church tells us NOT TO EAT OR DRINK ANYTHING FROM TWELVE O'CLOCK AT NIGHT until after we have received Holy Communion.

"So be very careful not to take a drink during the night or before you go to Holy Mass."

When You Awaken

"As soon as you awaken in the morning, tell Jesus that you are happy because YOU ARE GOING TO RECEIVE HIM IN THE HOLY HOST SO SOON.

"Tell Him that you want to be more holy.

"And ask Him to let you have more of His Love and Truth in you."

* * *

After You Arise

"When you arise, take time to say your morning prayers. And be sure to say the Our Father, the Hail Mary and Acts of Faith, Hope and Love.

"Until Holy Mass begins, prepare for it quietly, thinking all the time of Jesus and asking Jesus' Mother to watch over you as she watched over Jesus.

"Pray also to Saint Joseph.

"And tell Saint Joseph that you want him to take care of you as he took care of Jesus and His holy Mother.

"Now would you like to ask some questions?"

Tom asked: "What prayers shall we say at the beginning of Holy Mass?"

❧ ❧ ❧ ❧

THE BEGINNING OF HOLY MASS

THEIR father answered: "At the beginning of Holy Mass, it is always well to say many Acts of Faith, Hope, Love and Contrition. For these Acts are very pleasing to God and will help to prepare you for the coming of Jesus in The Holy Host.

PAGE 6

PAGE 7

The Middle of Holy Mass

"Or if you wish, you may offer the prayers given in your prayer-book for 'The Beginning of Holy Mass.'

" 'The First Part of Holy Mass,' in **Book Four** of 'A Little Child's First Communion' also tells you what to do at the beginning of Holy Mass.

"Let us read pages 38 and 39 together.

"And then I am sure that you will also want to read again what **Book Four** tells about the MIDDLE OF HOLY MASS when the bread and wine are changed into The Body and Blood of Jesus. This is told on pages 28, 29, 30 and 31."

THE CONSE-CRATION

AFTER Tom and Ann and their father had read the pages from **Book Four** telling about Holy Mass, Tom asked: "What prayers shall we say at the time the priest changes the bread and wine into The Body and Blood of Jesus?"

Their father answered: "During this part of Holy Mass, you may offer the prayers for The Consecration which you will find in your prayer-book. Or you may offer prayers in your own words.

"But at The Consecration, when Jesus is present offering to His Father FOR US His Own Body and His Own Blood with all of His great, great love and obedience,

PAGE 8

DO NOT FORGET TO THANK JESUS AND TO OFFER HIM YOUR OWN LOVE AND OBEDIENCE."

PAGE 9

"The stories 'At Holy Mass with Jesus,' 'Some Important Advice,' and 'Why We Offer Prayers through Jesus,' which are all in **Book Four**, will also help you to know what to do at this sacred time. Read these stories. You will find them on pages 32, 33, 34, 35 and 36."

"MY LORD AND MY GOD!"

"WHEN the bell rings and the priest holds up high The Holy Host, I always do what Pope Pius X said that he would like to have us do at that time. I look up at The Holy Host and say with great faith and love:

" 'MY LORD AND MY GOD!'

"At this sacred time, I am sure that you, too, will say this prayer, and that you will also want to speak to Jesus and tell Him all that you would have told Him if you had been standing near The Cross when He was dying upon It."

✝ ✝ ✝ ✝

PAGE 10

PAGE 11

"JESUS MY GOD, I THANK YOU"

"WHEN the priest holds up high the gold cup in which Jesus is present under the appearance of wine, I look up and say: " 'JESUS, MY GOD, I THANK YOU.'

"For I never forget that Jesus is present at The Consecration in Holy Mass to offer Himself to His Father, FOR US — His Own Body and Blood, with all of His great love and obedience, AS HE DID WHEN HE WAS DYING UPON THE CROSS.

"And now that you understand what Jesus is doing for us at this sacred time, I am sure that you, too, will want to say, 'Jesus, my God, I thank You.' "

"LORD I AM NOT WORTHY"

"A LITTLE while after The Consecration, you will hear the priest saying in quite a loud voice the Latin words:

" 'DOMINE NON SUM DIGNUS.'

"Then it is well to say the English words which have the very same meaning as these Latin words. The English words are:

" 'LORD, I AM NOT WORTHY.'

"Would you like to ask any other question?"

Ann asked: "How shall we know when to go to the altar-rail? And what shall we do when we are going to receive Jesus in Holy Communion?"

PAGE 12

RECEIVING HOLY COMMUNION

THEIR father replied: "When the priest says: 'Domine non sum dignus,' the bell usually rings three times.

"Soon after this, you should go to the altar-rail to receive Holy Communion.

"**And when you go to the altar-rail, keep your hands together and look down** so that you will not see anything which will make you forget that JESUS IS COMING TO YOU.

"When you are kneeling at the altar-rail and the priest brings The Holy Host to you, **hold your head up, open your mouth and place your tongue upon**

your lower lip. Then the priest will lay The Holy Host upon your tongue.

"**When you receive The Holy Host, swallow It at once.** If a little piece should stick to the upper part of your mouth, loosen It with your tongue. But of course do not touch The Holy Host with your fingers.

"Return to your place again, keeping your hands together and looking down, so that you will not see anything which will cause you to think of it instead of Jesus."

SPEAKING WITH JESUS

"JESUS, your God, is within you.

"He loves you and you love Him.

"SPEAK TO HIM. And as you learned in **Book Four**, THANK HIM FOR COMING TO YOU. Tell Him that you want to grow more and more like Him.

"ASK HIM TO LET YOU HAVE MORE OF HIS LOVE AND TRUTH IN YOU.

"And also ask Him for all the other good things you would like.

"Pray for the Pope who is the head of Jesus' Church on earth. And pray for the bishops and priests of Jesus' Church.

THANKING JESUS

"Then pray for good things for other people. And be sure to ask for many good things for mother and father."

🕯 🕯 🕯 🕯

"Of COURSE, before leaving the church, thank Jesus for HIS VISIT, HIS LOVE, and HIS MANY, MANY GIFTS. And tell Him that you will return to receive Him soon again.

"Then say these little prayers which I found in the holiest of all books and have written on this card for you.

"And now, good-night, Tom and Ann."

PAGE 16

Little Prayers of Praise

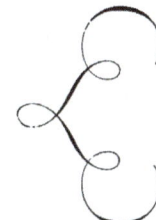 For TOM and ANN from FATHER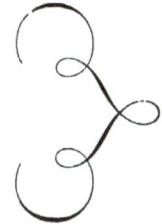

"O GIVE **THANKS** UNTO THE LORD FOR HE IS GOOD!"

* * *

"I WILL **PRAISE** THEE, O LORD MY GOD, WITH MY WHOLE HEART, AND **I WILL GLORIFY THY NAME, FOREVER.**"

* * *

"I WILL **SING** TO THE LORD, WHO GIVETH ME GOOD THINGS, AND I WILL **SING** TO THE NAME **OF THE LORD MOST HIGH.**"

* * *

"**HEARKEN** TO THE VOICE OF MY PRAYER, **O MY KING AND MY GOD;** FOR TO THEE WILL I **PRAY,** O LORD."

PAGE 18

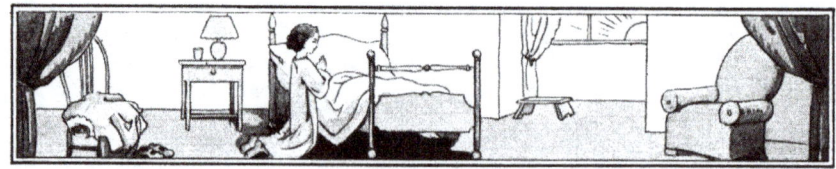

A Test: Holy Communion

Find the parts of sentences in A and B that go together.

FROM MIDNIGHT BEFORE HOLY COMMUNION

A

Jesus' Church tells you ....

As soon as you awaken in the morning, tell Jesus ....

When you arise, ...

Until Holy Mass begins, ...

B

.... that you are happy because He is coming to you so soon.

.... not to eat or drink anything from 12 o'clock at night until after you have received Holy Communion.

.... prepare for Holy Mass thinking all the time of Jesus.

.... kneel and say your morning prayers.

PAGE 19

DURING MASS BEFORE HOLY COMMUNION

A

At the beginning of Holy Mass, ...

When the priest holds up The Holy Host, I look up and say: ....

When the priest holds up the gold cup in which Jesus is present under the appearance of wine, I look up and say: ....

B

.... "Jesus, my God, I thank You."

.... offer the prayers given in your prayer-book for the beginning of The Mass, or say Acts of Faith, Hope, Love and Contrition.

.... "My Lord and my God."

PAGE 20

AT THE TIME OF HOLY COMMUNION

A

When the priest says: "Domine non sum dignus," ....

When the time comes for Holy Communion, walk to the altar-rail, looking ....

When the priest brings The Holy Host to you, ...

Do not touch ....

B

.... The Holy Host with your fingers.

.... down and keeping your hands together.

.... hold your head up, open your mouth, and place your tongue upon your lower lip.

.... I say the English words: "Lord, I am not worthy."

PAGE 21

AFTER HOLY COMMUNION

A

Return to your place, looking ....

Jesus, your God, is within you. Tell ....

Ask Jesus to give ....

Say Acts of ....

B

.... you many good things for yourself and others.

.... Faith, Hope and Love (Book Four, page 41).

.... down and keeping your hands together.

.... Him that you want to grow more and more like Him.

✦ ✦ ✦

Read the sentences to someone at home and ask if you have put them together right.

PAGE 22

THE HOLY HOST

Music by
CORNELIA S. CRANE

Je - sus in the Host so Ho - ly,

Thou wilt come to me so low - ly

Je - sus how I long for Thee

Come sweet Je - sus, come to me.

TOM AND ANN OFFER FLOWERS TO JESUS

THEIR father said to Tom and Ann:

"When Jesus comes to you in Holy Communion, would you like to offer Him a **bouquet** of flowers?"

They said that they would like to do this if he would tell them what flowers to offer.

Their father answered:

"For the **rose** in your bouquet you may say this prayer:

" 'JESUS, MY GOD, GIVE ME MORE OF YOUR LOVE EACH DAY.'

Little Prayers to Jesus

"For the **lily of the valley**  you may say:

" 'JESUS, YOU LOVE ME; MAKE ME MORE AND MORE LIKE YOU IN HOLINESS.'

"For the **forget-me-not**  say:

" 'MY JESUS, HELP ME NEVER, NEVER TO FORGET YOU.'

"For the **violet**  you may say:

" 'JESUS, MY MODEL, I WANT TO BE LIKE YOU: HELP ME NEVER TO BE PROUD.'

"For the **ferns**  say this prayer:

" 'JESUS MOST TRUE, HELP ME ALWAYS TO BE TRUE.' "

PAGE 25

SOME STORIES TOLD BY JESUS

"WHEN Jesus was living upon this earth, He told many stories to those who followed Him. For Jesus often used stories when He was teaching the people.

"Some of the stories Jesus told are about HEAVEN.

"And now perhaps you would like to hear some of these stories."

Tom and Ann said that they would like very much to hear them.

And these are the stories their father told Tom and Ann that evening:

⚡ ⚡ ⚡ ⚡

"Heaven, you know, is Jesus' kingdom.
"And when we die, of course we all want to be in heaven.

"Jesus Himself tells us that Holy Communion prepares us for heaven.

"For He said:

"'I AM THE BREAD OF LIFE...

"'IF ANY MAN EAT OF THIS BREAD,

"'HE SHALL LIVE FOREVER.'

"When Jesus said, 'I Am The Bread of Life,' He meant that in Holy Communion He Himself becomes our BREAD.

"And when Jesus said that those who ate of THIS BREAD would live FOREVER, He meant that those who received Holy Communion lovingly all their lives here on earth WOULD THEN BE IN HIS KINGDOM FOREVER."

"These are some other stories about heaven that Jesus Himself told us.

"'THE KINGDOM OF HEAVEN is like to a merchant seeking good pearls; who, when he had found ONE PEARL OF GREAT PRICE, went his way, and SOLD ALL that he had, and BOUGHT IT.'"

"'Again, THE KINGDOM OF HEAVEN is like to a net cast into the sea, and gathering together of all kinds of fishes; which, when it was filled, they drew out, and sitting by the shore, THEY CHOSE OUT THE GOOD INTO VESSELS, but the bad they cast forth.

"'SO SHALL IT BE AT THE END OF THE WORLD. The angels shall go out, and shall separate the wicked from among the just.'"

PAGE 27

A Test: What Is It?

It is like a pearl of great price.
It is like a net cast into the sea.
It is Jesus' kingdom.
It lasts forever. *What is it?*

"If any man eat of This Bread he shall live forever."
It prepares us for Jesus' kingdom.
When we receive It, Jesus comes to us.
When we receive It, Jesus gives us of His Holiness. *What is it?*

It will be the last thing to happen on earth.
The angels will separate the good from the bad.
The good will be full of joy.
The wicked will be very sad. *What is it?*

VISITS TO JESUS

WHEN the priest was talking with Tom and Ann on their First Communion Day, he said to them: "After Holy Communion, the priest places a gold cup in a little home on the altar. And in this gold cup some HOLY HOSTS ARE KEPT.

"This little home has a door which is always locked except when the priest opens it.

"It is called THE TABERNACLE.

"So whenever you go to Jesus' Church, you can visit Jesus in The Holy Host.

"And you should genuflect when you come in and before you leave. For to genuflect is one way to show honor to Jesus."

PAGE 28

PAGE 29

Showing Honor to Jesus

Tom said to Ann: "Let us visit Jesus in The Holy Host every day."

And the priest said: "May God bless you both."

A Project

Ask someone at home to show you how to genuflect correctly. Then teach some younger child how to show honor to Jesus by genuflecting.

FOR YOUR COMMUNION NOTEBOOK
OR PROJECT PAGES

Draw the flowers of the bouquet you offered to Jesus. If you cannot draw the flowers cut them out of seed catalogues or magazines.

Under each flower write its name and the prayer you said.

The Sacred Vessels

C-i-b-o-r-i-u-m — In the picture, the large gold cup with the cover beside it is called a *ciborium*. The small hosts are placed in the ciborium to be consecrated.

After the Consecration, The Holy Hosts which have not been given to the people at Holy Communion are kept in the ciborium. And the ciborium is kept in the tabernacle.

C-h-a-l-i-c-e — The other gold cup is called a *chalice*. The chalice is to hold the wine which is to be consecrated. And after The Consecration, Jesus is present under the appearance of wine.

P-a-t-e-n — The little gold plate near the chalice is called a *paten*. On the paten is a large host. The large host becomes A Holy Host when the priest uses the power Jesus gave him. It is This Host which the priest holds up high.

Draw a ciborium, a chalice and a paten.

A RECORD OF HOLY COMMUNIONS

On both inside covers of your First Communion Notebook draw lines one inch apart from top to bottom and then from side to side, thus covering each page with one-inch squares.

Each time you receive Holy Communion, draw a flower in one square. Draw the flower which shows what prayer you have offered most often to Jesus.

Try to find a picture showing Jesus teaching little children, a picture showing a child visiting Jesus in The Holy Host, and a picture showing children receiving Holy Communion.

Under each picture write a sentence explaining what the picture tells.

PAGE 31

ONE DAY, after their First Holy Communion, when Tom and Ann were talking again with their father, Ann said: "Now we know about four Sacraments. But there are seven. Please tell us about the other three Sacraments."

OTHER SACRAMENTS

WHEN WE ARE VERY SICK

THEIR father answered: "There is one Sacrament which the priest gives us when we are very sick.

"Suppose that I were very sick.

"Then mother would send for the priest, and the priest would come bringing holy oil. With the holy oil he would anoint my eyes, my ears, my nostrils, my mouth and my hands. And during the anointing, the priest would pray to God to forgive all the sins that I had ever committed in using my eyes, my ears, my nostrils, my mouth and my hands.

"Then I would have received the Sacrament called Extreme Unction.

PAGE 32

PAGE 33

The Sacrament of Extreme Unction

"I am telling you now only a little about the Sacrament of Extreme Unction. But later in your life you will learn more about this Sacrament, and just what mother or you or I should do to be ready for the priest if he were coming to our house to give the Sacrament of Extreme Unction."

✝ ✝ ✝

What Sacrament can a person receive only when he is very sick?

When anyone is receiving the Sacrament of Extreme Unction, what does the priest use when he is anointing him?

When anyone is receiving the Sacrament of Extreme Unction, what parts of his body are anointed?

When the priest is anointing anyone, what does he ask God to do for that person?

The Sacrament of Matrimony

"THERE are two other Sacraments.

"MOTHER AND I RECEIVED THE SACRAMENT CALLED MATRIMONY WHEN WE WERE MARRIED.

"You will learn much more about the Sacrament of Matrimony when you are older. For good Catholics always try to find out all that Jesus' Church teaches about every Sacrament.

"And Jesus' Church tells us some very important things about marriage. For it tells those who are going to be married and those who are married what they must do if they want to have God's blessing for themselves and for their children.

PAGE 35

The Sacrament of Holy Orders

"ANOTHER Sacrament of Jesus' Church is called Holy Orders. And all of Jesus' priests have received this Sacrament.

"FOR TO BECOME ONE OF JESUS' PRIESTS IT IS NECESSARY TO RECEIVE THE SACRAMENT CALLED HOLY ORDERS.

"Jesus' bishops and priests are given the power to offer Holy Mass. They are given the power to forgive our sins. And it is through Jesus' bishops and priests that we receive all the other Sacraments.

"So you see how grateful we should be to Jesus for giving us the Sacrament of Holy Orders."

A WORD GAME

"Now YOU know the names of all the Sacraments of Jesus' Church. How many are there?"

"Seven," answered Ann.

"To help you remember the names of the Sacraments, I will give you a word game. Here is a card with the names of the seven Sacraments **written backward.**

> msitpaB   tsirahcuE yloH   sredrO yloH
> noitamrifnoC   ecnaneP   ynomirtaM
> noitcnU emertxE

"Turn the words around and write them in your First Communion Notebook.

"Begin each word with a capital letter.

"When you have finished, give the card to mother and ask her to play the game."

PAGE 36

Child's Name:

....

— can do the test on page 3 correctly.

— can do "A Test: Holy Communion" on pages 18, 19, 20 and 21 correctly.

— knows the little prayers on pages 23 and 24.

— can say or sing the verse, "The Holy Host."

— can name the seven Sacraments and tell when we receive each one of them.

— has kept a neat First Communion Notebook or has finished some neat project pages approved by the teacher.

— can tell in a child's own words what *Book Six* teaches about preparing for Holy Communion.

— can tell how we are to act when we are going to the altar-rail to receive Holy Communion; how we are to act when we are receiving Holy Communion; how we are to act after we have received Holy Communion.

— knows a prayer to say when the priest holds up high The Holy Host.

— knows a prayer to say after the priest has consecrated the wine.

— knows the prayers on page 17.

— can tell two stories about Jesus' kingdom.

— can genuflect correctly.

— knows what this book teaches about Holy Orders and Matrimony.

....

Parent's Signature

www.ingramcontent.com/pod-product-compliance
Lightning Source LLC
Chambersburg PA
CBHW082114230426
43671CB00015B/2697